GOD'S COVENANT

With YOU

FOR DELIVERANCE & FREEDOM

JOHN ECKHARDT

CHARISMA
HOUSE

Most CHARISMA HOUSE BOOK GROUP products are available at special quantity discounts for bulk purchase for sales promotions, premiums, fund-raising, and educational needs. For details, write Charisma House Book Group, 600 Rinehart Road, Lake Mary, Florida 32746, or telephone (407) 333-0600.

GOD'S COVENANT WITH YOU FOR DELIVERANCE AND FREEDOM
    by John Eckhardt
Published by Charisma House
Charisma Media/Charisma House Book Group
600 Rinehart Road
Lake Mary, Florida 32746
www.charismahouse.com

Cover design by Justin Evans
Design Director: Bill Johnson

Visit the author's website at www.johneckhardtministries.com.

Library of Congress Cataloging-in-Publication Data:

Eckhardt, John, 1957-

God's covenant with you for deliverance and freedom / John Eckhardt. -- First edition.

    pages cm

Includes bibliographical references and index.

ISBN 978-1-62136-579-2 (trade paper : alk. paper) -- ISBN 978-1-62136-580-8 (e-book : alk. paper)

1. Spiritual warfare. 2. Spiritual warfare--Biblical teaching. 3. Liberty--Religious aspects--Christianity. 4. Covenants--Religious aspects--Christianity. 5. Bible. Leviticus--Criticism, interpretation, etc. 6. Bible. Deuteronomy--Criticism, interpretation, etc. I. Title.

BV4509.5.E24 2014

231.7'6--dc23

                                        2013049473

While the author has made every effort to provide accurate telephone numbers and Internet addresses at the time of publication, neither the publisher nor the author assumes any responsibility for errors or for changes that occur after publication.

This publication is translated in Spanish under the title *El pacto de Dios con usted para su rescate y liberación*, copyright © 2014 by John Eckhardt, published by Casa Creación, a Charisma Media company. All rights reserved.

First edition

14 15 16 17 18 — 9 8 7 6 5 4 3 2 1

CONTENTS

    DEMONIC OPPRESSION 30

    HOW DO YOU GET A SPIRIT OF REJECTION? 30

    WHAT ARE THE SIGNS AND SYMPTOMS OF
    A SPIRIT OF REJECTION? 36

    REJECTED BY GOD? 37

    WHAT FREES YOU FROM A SPIRIT OF
    REJECTION? 41

    REJECTION MUST GO! 46

    PRAYERS FOR DELIVERANCE FROM REJECTION ... 47

4   "LOOSE THYSELF"—SELF-DELIVERANCE 49

    SELF-DELIVERANCE 49

    LOOSE THYSELF FROM THE PAST 50

    LOOSE THYSELF FROM UNGODLY SOUL TIES 53

    LOOSE YOUR MEMORY 54

    LOOSE THYSELF FROM UNFORGIVENESS AND
    BITTERNESS 54

    LOOSE YOUR EMOTIONS 55

    LOOSE THYSELF FROM OCCULT BONDAGE 56

    LOOSE YOUR MIND 56

    LOOSE YOUR WILL 57

    LOOSE YOUR SEXUAL CHARACTER 58

    LOOSE THYSELF FROM EVIL INHERITANCE 59

    LOOSE THYSELF FROM FEAR 59

CHAPTER 1
DELIVERANCE AND THE COVENANT OF MERCY

Many are the afflictions of the righteous, but
the LORD delivers him out of them all.

—PSALM 34:19

WHEN YOU READ the Old Testament and the prophets, the main theme is that Israel had broken covenant with God. Israel was guilty of spiritual adultery, Israel had broken the covenant, and there was a curse or judgment coming against them. God said that there were blessings and curses in the covenant. If you kept the covenant, you would be blessed. If you break it, you will be cursed. So every time the Lord sent a prophet, the prophet was coming as a covenant messenger of Jehovah to warn Israel of covenant violations to call them back to covenant. Israel killed the covenant messengers of God, and God promised to avenge the blood of the prophets. The consistent covenant violation finally resulted in the destruction of the temple (as Jesus prophesied in Matthew 24) and their entire system because of broken covenant.

This is the whole theme of Scripture: God is faithful; man is unfaithful. God keeps covenant; man breaks covenant. When man breaks covenant, God judges him. But in the midst of broken covenant one of the things we can count on is that there is always a remnant of people who are faithful to covenant. An example of this is God telling Elijah in 1 Kings 19:18, "Yet I have reserved seven thousand in Israel, all whose knees have not bowed to Baal, and every mouth that has not kissed him." Those seven thousand had been faithful to God and to the covenant; they had not worshiped idols.

In Scripture those who remained faithful are known as the

1

remnant. We need to understand *remnant* in terms of covenant. God promised that He would save this remnant, and because of His covenant promises with Abraham mercy was always extended to Israel. Even though God would judge them, He would never completely destroy them. God always remembered His covenant promise to Abraham. God told Abraham that through his seed all the families of the earth will be blessed. Every time they got in trouble and broke covenant God would judge, but then His mercy would come and God would save them, deliver them, and restore them.

Deliverance out of trouble is a form of God's mercy being enacted because of covenant. If it wasn't for the mercy of God, every covenant violation that we commit today would cause us to be destroyed. Our actions outside of God's plans for our lives put us in violation of the covenant and opens us up to all kinds of evil and torment from the enemy.

The covenant provides certain benefits, including protection and deliverance. People living outside the covenant do not have these benefits and therefore are susceptible to the work of the enemy. Sin is an open door for demons, and those who do not enjoy the benefits of redemption and forgiveness are more susceptible to demonic intrusion into their lives. Those who walk in covenant enjoy the blessing of forgiveness from sin, and the operation of demons is limited and hindered.

Redemption is the solution to the problem of sin. Those who engage in sin will have open doors for demons to come in and operate. Those outside of covenant live in darkness, which is the realm of Satan and demons. Those who walk in covenant live in the light. Darkness is the realm of demons, and light is the realm of God.

But God has created a way for us to be delivered out of all our troubles. The Bible says, "Many are the afflictions of the righteous, but the LORD delivers him out of them all" (Ps. 34:19). This deliverance is God's mercy extended to those who are in covenant with Him. When God's covenant people call, He hears them and answers them.

WE ARE GOD'S COVENANT PEOPLE

You and I are the seed of Abraham through faith in Jesus Christ. Therefore God's covenant to Abraham is also with us. (See Genesis 15.) So now the mercy of God comes upon your life through Jesus Christ. When the Bible says the mercy of the Lord endures forever, it never ends, and it is steadfast, it simply means that from generation to generation to generation there will be a people God will have mercy on, be kind to, show tenderness to, and forgive. There will always be a generation, because there is always a seed of Abraham. Now through faith we are the seed of Abraham, which means that you must understand, trust, and believe in the mercy of God. God's loyalty to covenant extends His mercy into your life. God is merciful to you because of covenant, and if you have a covenant through Jesus Christ with God, you can expect His mercy to be upon your life.

Abraham was called the friend of God, which means he had a covenant relationship with God. He was a covenant friend, which means he was committed to God and God was committed to him—to take care of him and preserve him and then take care of His seed from generation to generation.

DELIVERANCE IS AN EXPRESSION OF GOD'S COVENANTAL MERCY AND COMPASSION

When Jesus came, He came to bring judgment, but He also came to bring mercy—salvation, deliverance, and healing, which are all manifestations of God's mercy. Sometimes we think that our deliverance and healing are based on what we do and don't do, but our deliverance and healing are based on the mercy of God, God's loving-kindness, and God's covenantal loyalty. God is connected with you, and He has made a covenant with you through Jesus Christ.

Let's look at how this is possible through the prophetic word released in Zacharias, John the Baptist's father. The Bible says in Luke 1:67–72 (emphasis added):

> Now his father Zacharias was filled with the Holy Spirit, and prophesied, saying: "Blessed is the Lord God of Israel, for He has visited and redeemed His people, and has raised up a horn of salvation for us in the house of His servant David, as He spoke by the mouth of His holy prophets, who have been since the world began, that we [Israel] should be saved from our enemies and from the hand of all who hate us, *to perform the mercy promised to our fathers and to remember His holy covenant...*"

This is saying that salvation came to Israel because God remembered His covenant with Abraham and that God was about to perform the mercy promised to Abraham.

In verse 73 it goes on to say, "...the oath which He swore to our father Abraham: to grant us that we, being delivered from the hand of our enemies, might serve Him without fear, in holiness and righteousness before Him all the days of our life."

So we see mercy connected with covenant. Within the covenant there is mercy, loving-kindness, compassion, forgiveness, healing, deliverance, redemption.

Jesus was the promise and the fulfillment of the covenant. You can see that His ministry on earth was filled with the works of the covenant. In John 10:31–38 Jesus talks about the works that He was doing. He was healing the sick and casting out devils, doing the works of His Father, and many of the Jews did not understand what was taking place. But He made it clear in this passage that these were the works of the Father. He made it clear that what He was doing was not done on His own. What He did was an extension of the Father—healing, delivering, rescuing, and setting people free. He was not doing those things in His own power. He was doing them by the anointing and power of the Spirit of God. He was fulfilling the covenant God the Father made with Abraham. God's mercy was being revealed through the works of Christ:

- Healing the sick
- Casting out devils
- Raising the dead
- Cleansing the lepers
- Opening blind eyes
- Unstopping deaf ears
- Loosing dumb tongues

God's mercy was being manifested through Jesus—God's mercy, compassion, loving-kindness on Israel; His love in saving them, healing them, delivering them, and restoring them. Jesus demonstrated to them—and to us—that He is the representation of God, who is concerned about people who are hurting, sick, wounded, bleeding, and dying. Jesus was a visible manifestation of mercy—mercy in action. All because of God's covenant with Abraham, this same manifestation of mercy now comes to you.

GOD IS FAITHFUL TO HIS COVENANT

God cannot break covenant. It is impossible for God to lie. He cannot go back on that word. God cannot lie. God is absolutely faithful and committed to covenant. This is one of the essential aspects of God. He is loyal to His people. He will not ever violate covenant. He will not betray His people.

We can trust and rely on God's covenant because He is committed to His promises. When a covenant is made, the person enacting the covenant would swear by someone higher than himself. This was so that if the covenant was ever broken, that person would be judged and held accountable to the person higher than him. When God first established His covenant with Abraham, He swore by an oath, and since He could swear by no one higher, He swore by Himself.

> For when God made a promise to Abraham, because He could swear by no greater, He swore by Himself.
> —HEBREWS 6:13

God is the highest. There is no one greater than Him. This means we can absolutely trust, rely upon, and depend upon our covenant with God. God cannot lie. He will remain faithful to His Word and His covenant of mercy.

By Jesus coming to earth and bringing salvation and deliverance, we see the personification of God's faithfulness. From the time of Abraham, Isaac, and Jacob, through Moses, David, and the prophets, God had promised to send a deliverer. His name was Jesus, "for He will save His people from their sins" (Matt. 1:21).

That is why in the Gospels we see people approach Jesus with their issues, saying, "Son of David, have mercy upon me." They understood that when the Messiah—the Son of David—came, He would extend God's mercy to Israel. We see that in the prophecy of Zacharias that I pointed out in the section above.

Zacharias was declaring that the Messiah has come and Israel would see through Jesus the greatest manifestation of God's faithfulness and mercy ever known to man—salvation. His incarnation was the manifestation of eternal salvation and eternal redemption. So not only would He perform miracles for Israel, but He would also ensure their eternal redemption, salvation, forgiveness, and bring them into the kingdom.

MERCY COMES TO THE GENTILES

Contrary to what we may realize, Jesus was not a minister to everyone. His primary purpose was to fulfill God's covenant promises made to Abraham and to Israel, to confirm them, to fulfill them to extend mercy to Israel, to save the remnant.

Jeremiah 31:31–34 says:

> I will make a new covenant with the house of Israel and with the house of Judah—not according to the covenant that I made with their fathers in the day that I took them by the hand to lead them out of the land of Egypt, My covenant which they broke, though I was a husband to them, says the LORD. But this is the covenant that I will make with the house of Israel after those days, says the LORD: I will put My law in their minds, and write it on their hearts; and I will be their God, and they shall be My people. No more shall every man teach his neighbor, and every man his brother, saying, "Know the LORD," for they all shall know Me, from the least of them to the greatest of them, says the LORD. For I will forgive their iniquity, and their sin I will remember no more.

His primary purpose was to fulfill God's covenant promises made to Abraham and to Israel, to confirm them, to fulfill them to extend mercy to Israel, to save the remnant. He did not come to minister to Jews *and* Gentiles. When Gentiles came to Him for ministry, He was shocked at their faith.

We see this proven in the story of the Gentile woman who came to Jesus and asked Him to heal her daughter. Jesus said, "I was not sent except to the lost sheep of the house of Israel.... It is not good to take the children's bread and throw it to the little dogs" (Matt. 15:25–26). That does not seem like a very compassionate or merciful response, to call someone a dog. She persisted and said, "Yes, Lord, yet even the little dogs eat the crumbs which fall from their masters' table" (v. 27). Basically she was saying, "I don't want what belongs to the people of God. I just want what they don't want." Understand that God could have healed and delivered everybody in Israel, but Israel wasn't taking all that God had. So there were some crumbs available. Crumbs are what's left over. And because Israel left behind so much of what God had for them, Jesus healed her daughter.

People may not understand why Jesus responded to her the way He did. You have to remember that she was a Gentile and was not in covenant with God. She had no right to claim mercy. She had no covenant, no relationship with God. Mercy is connected to covenant. When you are in covenant with God, you can receive mercy. Mercy is available to you.

Let's take a look at another story in Luke 17:12–18:

> Then as He entered a certain village, there met Him ten
> men who were lepers, who stood afar off. And they lifted
> up their voices and said, "Jesus, Master, have mercy on
> us!" So when He saw them, He said to them, "Go, show
> yourselves to the priests." And so it was that as they went,
> they were cleansed. And one of them, when he saw that
> he was healed, returned, and with a loud voice glorified
> God, and fell down on his face at His feet, giving Him
> thanks. And he was a Samaritan. So Jesus answered and
> said, "Were there not ten cleansed? But where are the
> nine? Were there not any found who returned to give
> glory to God except this foreigner?"

I believe that this story of the one Samaritan leper who came back is in the Bible to show that Israel received so much mercy from God, but they didn't appreciate it. The Samaritan (a Gentile) was thankful. The outsiders are more thankful than the insiders. The insiders take it for granted. The Samaritan came back and thanked Jesus. He was glad to get healed. He understood that he wasn't a Jew, that he wasn't in covenant, but he still got healed. The other nine went on their merry way. Many of those who are in covenant are often not thankful for the mercy of God. They take it for granted.

Only the remnant of the house of Israel received Jesus's ministry and His fulfillment of the covenant. The rest of Israel hardened their hearts. So God extended His mercy to the Gentiles. That's us! We will get saved. We will get healed. We will get delivered. It was always God's plan that His mercy would go to the nations or the Gentiles. Romans 15:8–9: "Now I say that Jesus Christ has become a servant to the circumcision [to the Jews] for the truth of God, to confirm the promises made to the fathers [Abraham, Jacob, and Isaac], and that the Gentiles might glorify God for His mercy."

But remember mercy is connected to covenant. In order for the Gentiles to receive the mercy of God, God had to make a new covenant.

THE NEW COVENANT MAKES GOD'S MERCY AVAILABLE TO YOU

Jesus sat down with His disciples on Passover night and took the bread and the cup and said, "This cup is the new covenant in My blood, which is shed for you" (Luke 22:20). He made a new covenant with those twelve men, the new Israel of God. Now through the death of Christ we all come into a new covenant with God. So all those who were saved in Israel were saved through this new covenant. Then the Gentiles tapped into the covenant and began to receive mercy. Because you have a covenant through the blood of Jesus and you are a believer, mercy is extended to you!

Mercy is one of the most powerful forces there is. Mercy is connected to compassion and loving-kindness. When you have compassion and mercy on someone, you are willing to help them. You use your strength and power to help someone who is less fortunate, in need, and can't do it on their own.

In the Bible your bowels, your inward parts are connected to compassion. First John 3:17 says, "But whoso hath this world's good, and seeth his brother have need, and shutteth up his *bowels of compassion* from him, how dwelleth the love of God in him?" (KJV, emphasis added). This means compassion is a deep and powerful force that controls how you interact with another person. Your compassion for someone drives you or motivates you from the inside out to act on their behalf. When that deep emotion or feeling for others is shut off, you won't feel moved to do anything for them. Your inward parts are the center of your motivations for most of what you do. We often need deliverance in this area, the bowels, the inward parts. In 1 John 3:17 the Bible is essentially asking, "How can the love of God live in a person who is not *moved* to help someone in need?" It's not possible, because compassion and mercy are central to God's character. God is not just willing to help you; God is *moved* to help you. His mercy and compassion compel Him to come to your rescue and deliver you.

The Bible says this consistently about Jesus being moved with compassion when people came to Him in need of healing or deliverance from demonic spirits: "And when Jesus went out He saw a great multitude; and He was moved with compassion for them, and healed their sick" (Matt. 14:14).

- Jesus opened the eyes of the blind through compassion (Mark 10:46–52).
- Jesus cleansed the leper through compassion (Mark 1:41).
- The father brought his demonized child to Jesus for healing, and Jesus delivered his child through compassion (Mark 9:21–23).

- Jesus raised a child from the dead because of compassion
  and restored the son to his mother (Luke 7:12–15).

Jesus was moved with compassion when He saw the condition of
the lost sheep of the house of Israel (Matt. 9:36).

The Hebrew word for *mercy* is *checed*. It is translated in English
as "mercy, kindness, lovingkindness, goodness, kindly, merciful,
favour, good, goodliness, pity."[1] A related Hebrew word, *racham*,
speaks even more closely to the covenant mercy of God. It means
"to love, love deeply, have mercy, be compassionate, have tender affection, have compassion."[2]

You see it here in 2 Kings 13:23:

> But the LORD was gracious to them, had *compassion* [or
> mercy] on them, and regarded them, because of His cov-
> enant with Abraham, Isaac, and Jacob, and would not yet
> destroy them or cast them from His presence.
>
> —EMPHASIS ADDED

The word *compassion* in this verse is the same Hebrew word
racham used for *mercy* in other places in the Old Testament. (See
Exodus 33:19; Psalm 102:13; Proverbs 28:13; Isaiah 14:1; 30:18.) The
idea is that God's mercy, compassion, and pity are for His covenant
people. Mercy moves God and causes Him to act on our behalf. This
is why I say that deliverance from all our enemies is central to this
new covenant of mercy.

God didn't just feel sorry for us—that's not compassion. God was
moved by His mercy and did something about our situation. There
is a difference between feeling sorry for someone and having mercy
on someone. You can feel sorry for somebody and not do anything:
"Man, that's messed up. I really feel sorry for them." But you don't
want to get involved. That's not how God works. God got all the way
involved in our mess. When He saw His covenant people—the seed
of Abraham—sick, bound, demonized, poor, broken, controlled by

religious leaders, and taken advantage of, the covenantal nature of God came into manifestation on behalf of the children of His covenant friend Abraham. God was moved to do something about their situation. He is still moved today to rescue and deliver us even now. He sees our condition. He hears our groaning. He sees our bondage. He sent His Son to come in person to fulfill the awesome magnitude of His covenant of mercy and compassion extended to us—His covenant people, sons and daughters of Abraham.

HIS MERCY ENDURES FOREVER!

One of the greatest psalms in the Bible is Psalm 136. The rabbis call it the Great Halal. It says consistently, "Oh, give thanks to the LORD, for He is good! For His mercy endures forever." It lists all the things God did for Israel. What this passage is saying to you is that if you know God's mercy is on your life, you must be thankful for it. Thanksgiving is a response to the mercy of God. No one should make you praise and thank God. When you understand God's mercy, grace, forgiveness, healing, deliverance, and compassion on your life, every time you come in the house of God, you will put your hands together and praise God, lift your hands and thank Him. His mercy is from generation to generation. It never runs out. It never ends. His mercy endures forever. That is something to give God thanks for.

The word *endure* means: "to continue to exist…to remain firm under suffering or misfortune without yielding."[3] The word *forever* means: "for a limitless time, at all times, continually."[4] Hence, the meaning of each of these key words speaks to us of the powerful, firm, trustworthy, tenacious, never-ending love of God.

So as we discuss deliverance and you desire more and more to be set free, you need to believe that God is merciful, that God will heal you, that He will deliver you, that He has compassion, and that He is moved by your condition. Don't think that God doesn't care. God cares deeply and will move heaven and hell to come to your rescue. When you are being ministered to, know that it is a manifestation of the Spirit of God and the Father's great compassion, mercy, and loving-kindness toward you. The deliverances, the healings, the miracles—these are a manifestation of the Father's love flowing down and through you.

I believe that when we get a full revelation of covenant and God's mercy flowing through us, we will see more miracles in the body of Christ. When we yield to the Spirit of God and allow the Father's love and compassion to flow through us, we will see blind eyes opened, deaf ears unstopped, and the crippled walk. We cannot flow in or experience miracles, healing, and deliverance without the mercy of God. Every one of us should be channels of God's mercy to a lost and hurting world.

Nobody deserves healing and deliverance. It's God's covenant of mercy that extends those benefits to us. It is God's faithfulness to covenant that does this. It has nothing to do with any of us outside of our choice to receive Jesus. And Jesus did not come to judge us and beat up on us; He came to extend mercy to us and heal and deliver us. Thank God for His covenantal mercy upon our lives!

PRAYERS FOR THE MERCY AND DELIVERANCE OF GOD TO COME UPON YOUR LIFE

Hear me when I call, O God. Have mercy upon me and hear my prayer (Ps. 4:1).

Have mercy upon me, O Lord; for I am weak. Heal me, for my bones are troubled (Ps. 6:2).

Have mercy upon me, O Lord; consider the trouble I suffer from those who hate me, You who lift me up from the gates of death (Ps. 9:13).

Lord, show mercy to me, Your anointed, and give me great deliverance (Ps. 18:50).

Lord, let me see Your wonderful works in my life performed through Your compassion (Ps. 111:4).

Lord, You are plenteous in mercy and truth; let me experience Your abundant grace and mercy (Ps. 86:15).

God's mercy is on me, because I fear you (Luke 1:50).

In the Lord's great mercy He has not consumed or forsaken me (Neh. 9:31).

The Lord has helped me in remembrance of His mercy (Luke 1:54).

The Lord shows mercy to me, because I love Him and keep His commandments (Exod. 20:6).

I trust in the mercy of God (Ps. 13:5).

The mercy of the Most High will not be removed from me (Ps. 21:7).

The Lord remembers His tender mercies and His loving-kindness toward me, for they are from old (Ps. 25:6).

The Lord will turn Himself toward me and have mercy on me (Ps. 25:16).

The Lord will redeem me and be merciful to me (Ps. 26:11).

The Lord hears me and will have mercy on me. He is my helper (Ps. 30:10).

The eye of the Lord is on me because I fear Him and hope in His mercy (Ps. 33:18).

Blessed is the Lord, who has not turned away my prayers or His mercy from me (Ps. 66:20).

The Lord will show His mercy to me and will grant me His salvation (Ps. 85:7).

The Lord is good to me. His mercy is everlasting, and His truth endures to all my generations (Ps. 100:5).

The Lord redeems my life from destruction and crowns me with loving-kindness and tender mercies (Ps. 103:4).

The Lord has remembered His covenant and relented according to the multitude of His mercies (Ps. 106:45).

The Lord is merciful to me according to His word (Ps. 119:58).

In the Lord's mercy He has cut off my enemies and destroyed all those who afflicted my soul (Ps. 143:12).

Through the Lord's mercies I am not consumed (Lam. 3:22).

The Lord is rich in mercy toward me because of His great love toward me (Eph. 2:4).

In His mercy the Lord led me and redeemed. He has guided me in His strength to His holy habitation (Exod. 15:13).

The Lord is my tower of salvation and shows His mercy to me and my descendants forevermore (2 Sam. 22:51).

I will give thanks to the Lord, for He is good. His mercy endures forever (1 Chron. 16:34).

The Lord will make His face shine on me and will save me, for His mercies' sake (Ps. 31:16).

The God of mercy is my defense. I will sing praise to the Lord, who is my strength (Ps. 59:17).

The faithfulness and mercy of the Lord will be with me, and in His name my horn shall be exalted (Ps. 89:24).

The Lord will keep His mercy for me forever, and His covenant will stand firm with me (Ps. 89:28).

The Lord will satisfy me early with His mercy so that I may rejoice and be glad all my days (Ps. 90:14).

The mercy of the Lord will uphold me (Ps. 94:18).

The Lord's merciful kindness will be a comfort for me (Ps. 119:76).

The Lord's tender mercies are great toward me, and He will revive me with His judgments (Ps. 119:156).

I have the mercy of God because I confess and forsake my sins (Prov. 28:13).

Just as He forgave the children of Israel, He will pardon my iniquity according to the greatness of His mercy (Num. 14:19).

The Lord my God, the faithful God, keeps His covenant and mercy for a thousand generations because I love Him and keep His commandments (Deut. 7:9).

The Lord will arise and have mercy on me, for the time of my favor, yes, the set time, has come (Ps. 102:13).

My eyes look to the Lord my God until He has mercy on me (Ps. 123:2).

The Lord has made an everlasting covenant with me—the sure mercies of David (Isa. 55:3).

I will return to the Lord my God, for He is gracious and merciful, slow to anger, and of great kindness (Joel 2:13).

I will come boldly to the throne of grace to obtain mercy and help in my time of need (Heb. 4:16).

The Lord, in His manifold mercies, did not forsake me in the wilderness. He has led me and shown me the way I should go (Neh. 9:19).

According to His abundant mercy, the Lord will give me deliverers who will save me from the hand of my enemies (Neh. 9:27).

I shall neither hunger nor thirst, neither will heat or sun strike me, for the Lord has mercy on me and will lead me by the springs of water (Isa. 49:10).

The Lord my God will incline His ear and hear; He will open His eyes and see my desolations, for I present my supplications before Him because of His great mercies (Dan. 9:18).

The Lord will strengthen me. He will bring me back because He has mercy on me. I will not be cast aside. For He is the Lord my God, and He will hear me (Zech. 10:6).

CHAPTER 2
DELIVERANCE IS THE CHILDREN'S BREAD

Let the children be filled first, for it is not good to take
the children's bread and throw it to the little dogs.

—MARK 7:27

THE MINISTRY OF deliverance is an essential part of every church and every believer's life. It should be incorporated into every fellowship and embraced by all believers. The ministry of deliverance will strengthen you and prepare you for a greater manifestation of God's power. We need not fear a *valid* deliverance ministry.

Deliverance is from God and is part of the blessing of being in covenant with Him. It only destroys what is of the devil; it never destroys what is of the Holy Spirit. Since deliverance is a work of the Holy Spirit, it builds up the saints and edifies the church. It tears down the strongholds of the enemy, but builds up the work of God.

SPIRITUAL MALNUTRITION

And behold, a woman of Canaan came from that region and cried out to Him, saying, "Have mercy on me, O Lord, Son of David! My daughter is severely demon-possessed." …But He answered and said, "It is not good to take the children's bread and throw it to the little dogs."

—MATTHEW 15:22, 26

The woman was a Greek, a Syro-Phoenician by birth, and she kept asking Him to cast the demon out of her daughter. But Jesus said to her, "Let the children be filled

first, for it is not good to take the children's bread and
throw it to the little dogs."

—MARK 7:26–27

In both of these Scripture references Jesus refers to deliverance as
"the children's bread." The three words contain a revelation concerning the importance of deliverance ministry. Deliverance is bread
for the children of God. It is part of the spiritual diet from which
every believer has a right to partake. When deliverance is not part of
a believer's (or group of believers) diet, the result is spiritual malnutrition. I am convinced there are multitudes who are spiritually malnourished because they are not receiving the children's bread.

Bread, simply defined, is food or sustenance. *Sustenance* is
defined as "a means of support, maintenance, or subsistence…the
state of being sustained…something that gives support, endurance,
or strength."[1] Christians need bread to endure. Without such, there
will be fainting and weakness. The reason why so many believers
are weak and fainting is because they have not received deliverance,
which is the children's bread.

Both Matthew and Mark record the saying of Jesus: "the children's bread." However, several of Mark's words give us additional
insight: "Let the children be filled first." The word *filled* also means
to be satisfied. Just as the natural appetite cannot be satisfied without
bread, the spiritual appetite cannot be satisfied without deliverance.
The church has been trying to bring deliverance to the world while
ignoring the words of Jesus: "Let the children be filled first" (Mark
7:27). In other words, we cannot bring successful deliverance to the
world until we bring it to the church and we ourselves are delivered!

Bread is not a luxury food. It is a *staple food*. A *staple* is defined
as "something having widespread and constant use or appeal, the
sustaining or principal element."[2] When we refer to something as
being principle, we are saying it is a matter, or thing, of primary

importance. *Principal* is defined as "most important, consequential, or influential: chief."[3]

Since bread is a staple food and since deliverance is called "the children's bread," then we can conclude that deliverance is of primary importance to the life of the believer. It is a sustaining or principal element of our spiritual diet.

> He causes the grass to grow for the cattle, and vegetation for the service of man, that he may bring forth food from the earth, and wine that makes glad the heart of man, oil to make his face shine, and *bread which strengthens man's heart.*
>
> —PSALM 104:14–15, EMPHASIS ADDED

Bread strengths the heart. The Berkeley translation says, "and bread to improve man's health." Deliverance will certainly improve your health. You will not be healthy without partaking of this bread. The Jerusalem Bible says, "and bread to make them strong." Bread makes us strong. A lack of bread produces weakness, which is the result of malnutrition. The Harrison translation says, "with bread also, to refresh the human body."[4] Deliverance refreshes.

Every believer needs a refreshing. Deliverance, as part of the diet of any believer, will cause health, strength, and refreshing to come into the lives of those who partake of the children's bread.

FEED THE FLOCK

> The elders who are among you I exhort, I who am a fellow elder and a witness of the sufferings of Christ, and also a partaker of the glory that will be revealed: Shepherd the flock of God which is among you, serving as overseers, not by compulsion but willingly, not for dishonest gain but eagerly.
>
> —1 PETER 5:1–2

> Take heed therefore unto yourselves, and to all the flock,
> over the which the Holy Ghost hath made you overseers,
> *to feed the church of God*, which he hath purchased with
> his own blood.
>
> —Acts 20:28, kjv, emphasis added

The Bible in Basic English translates Acts 20:28 this way: "to give food to the church of God."

Since deliverance is the children's bread and the elders are commanded to feed the flock, then it is the responsibility of the pastors to minister and teach deliverance to the church of God.

Most pastors have been taught that feeding the church is simply preaching and teaching the Word of God. Most churches conduct Bible studies and preach sermons on Sundays as ways to feed the flock of God. However, there are many believers who have heard sermons, attended many Bible studies, and are still not satisfied.

They go from church to church and from conference to conference with "itching ears" trying to be filled by hearing another message. Although I believe that preaching and teaching are a major part of feeding the flock, I maintain that if deliverance is not a vital part of a church's ministry, the flock is not being properly fed.

In other words, preaching and teaching are a part of feeding the flock, but without deliverance, the feeding is incomplete. Feeding the church of God is more than sermons and Bible studies. If deliverance is the children's bread, then pastors are guilty of not adequately feeding the flock if they have neglected deliverance.

> And the word of the Lord came to me, saying, "Son of
> man, prophesy against the shepherds of Israel, prophesy
> and say to them, 'Thus says the Lord God to the shep-
> herds: "Woe to the shepherds of Israel who feed them-
> selves! Should not the shepherds feed the flocks?"'"
>
> —Ezekiel 34:1–2

Ezekiel gives a prophetic word against the shepherds who do not feed the flock. He pronounced a "woe" unto them. A woe is calamity and trouble coming upon the one over whom it is pronounced. Pastors who neglect to minister deliverance to the flock, providing for them bread, are in danger of the judgment of God. This is a sobering word when you consider that deliverance is a part of feeding the flock.

> You eat the fat and clothe yourselves with the wool; you slaughter the fatlings, but you do not feed the flock. The weak you have not strengthened, nor have you healed those who were sick, nor bound up the broken, nor brought back what was driven away, nor sought what was lost; but with force and cruelty you have ruled them.
>
> —EZEKIEL 34:3–4

This is obviously a reference to neglecting to minister deliverance to the people of God. Instead, the Lord points out the force and cruelty with which the flock has been treated. This is a reference to religious control and domination. The judgment of the Lord comes upon the shepherds who have not fed the flock but instead ruled them with harshness and severity.

GATHERING VS. SCATTERING

> So they were scattered because there was no shepherd; and they became food for all the beasts of the field when they were scattered.
>
> —EZEKIEL 34:5

The result of spiritual neglect from the shepherds of God's people: they are scattered. Could the neglect of deliverance cause the Lord's people to be scattered? The answer is a resounding yes!

In order to see this more clearly, I want to call your attention to the statement of our Lord Jesus in the Gospel of Matthew: "He who is not with Me is against Me, and he who does not gather with Me scatters abroad" (Matt. 12:30).

The context of these words spoken by our Lord are in reference to deliverance. The Pharisees had accused Him of casting out devils by Beelzubub, the prince of the devils (v. 24). Jesus responds by saying that He was casting out devils by the Spirit of God (v. 28). He then makes this statement: "…he who does not gather with Me scatters abroad" (v. 30). Jesus identifies deliverance as a gathering ministry. Those who oppose it are actually scattering.

This is exactly what Ezekiel prophesied to the shepherds. They had not fed the flock, and the result—they were scattered. Deliverance, the children's bread, causes the flock to gather; opposition to the ministry of deliverance causes them to scatter.

The people of God become prey to all the beasts of the field. Beasts represent evil spirits. Evil spirits actually feast upon the flocks because they have no shepherds feeding them with the bread of deliverance.

> My sheep wandered through all the mountains, and on every high hill; yes, My flock was scattered over the whole face of the earth, and no one was seeking or searching for them.
>
> —Ezekiel 34:6

When sheep don't receive deliverance, they will end up wandering and being scattered upon all the face of the earth. They will end up being a prey to the beasts of the field. The point to note is that the Lord does not blame the sheep; He places the responsibility on the shepherds.

I have often said that when the Lord sees His sheep in this condition, He looks for the shepherd. The shepherd is the one responsible for the condition of the flock. The shepherd is responsible to feed the flock and protect them from the ravages of the enemy.

> Therefore, you shepherds, hear the word of the Lord: "As I live," says the Lord God, "surely because My flock became a prey, and My flock became food for every beast of the field, because there was no shepherd, nor did My shepherds search for My flock, but the shepherds fed themselves and did not feed My flock."
>
> —Ezekiel 34:7–8

The Lord Is Your Shepherd

When you are malnourished, you are susceptible to sickness, disease, and other attacks upon the body and mind. Infection and disease often invade the body because it is too weak to fight off sickness. This is also true in the realm of the spirit.

When you don't have a proper spiritual diet, you are vulnerable to infection. You become vulnerable and susceptible to demonic attack. You become a victim of the wiles and schemes of the devil. This is why deliverance must be a part of your spiritual diet.

You must partake of the children's bread if you are to be strong enough to ward off the attacks of the enemy. The enemy will prey upon any weakness that results from spiritual malnutrition.

But don't lose hope if your church is not a church that operates in deliverance. The Lord has promised to rescue you and visit you with His presence. He will be your shepherd. (See Psalm 23.) You will not be left wanting for the vital sustenance of deliverance and protection from the attacks of the enemy.

> Therefore, O shepherds, hear the word of the Lord! Thus says the Lord God: "Behold, I am against the shepherds, and I will require My flock at their hand; I will cause them to cease feeding the sheep, and the shepherds shall feed themselves no more; for I will deliver My flock from their mouths, that they may no longer be food for them."
>
> —Ezekiel 34:9–10

The New English Bible says, "I will rescue my sheep from their jaws." The Moffat translation says, "I will rescue my flock from their greed." Since the shepherds did not feed the flock, the Lord will demand His flock back from them. He will rescue you Himself.

> Then she arose with her daughters-in-law that she might return from the country of Moab, for she had heard in the country of Moab that the LORD *had visited His people by giving them bread.*
>
> —RUTH 1:6, EMPHASIS ADDED

The Lord will personally visit you and give you the bread of deliverance. He has seen your famine, and He will have mercy upon you by sending deliverance, the children's bread. This is the day of visitation.

> Blessed is the Lord God of Israel, for He has visited and redeemed His people, and has raised up a horn of salvation for us in the house of His servant David.
>
> —LUKE 1:68–69

When visitation comes, deliverance (a horn of salvation) comes. When visitation comes, you will receive bread. You will be filled and satisfied. You will never truly be satisfied apart from a visitation of the Lord.

> So will I seek out My sheep and deliver them from all the places where they were scattered on a cloudy and dark day. And I will bring them out from the peoples and gather them from the countries, and will bring them to their own land; I will feed them on the mountains of Israel, in the valleys and in all the inhabited places of the country. I will feed them in good pasture...there they shall lie down in a good fold.
>
> —EZEKIEL 34:12–14

The Lord promises to visit you and give you bread. He will feed you in good pastures. There shall you lie in a good fold. The Lord is bringing you out of a bad fold and into a good fold where you can receive bread. He will visit you in the places where you have been driven and scattered and bring you back to lie down in green pastures. He will seek you out and visit you.

BALANCE BETWEEN DELIVERANCE AND THE WORD

> But He answered and said, "It is written, 'Man shall not live by bread alone, but by every word that proceeds from the mouth of God.'"
>
> —MATTHEW 4:4

Since I have used bread as a picture of deliverance, I want to reiterate that deliverance is a vital part of a believer's spiritual diet. Without deliverance you will be lacking in your diet, becoming spiritually malnourished. However, I must emphasize that deliverance, although a vital part, is only a part of being fed.

We cannot live by bread (deliverance) alone, but by every word that proceeds out of the mouth of God. Studying and receiving the Word of God is also a vital part of a proper spiritual diet. This includes anointed preaching and teaching and also prophecy, which is the word of the Lord. We need deliverance, but we also need the Word. We will not be strong without revelation, knowledge, prophesying, and doctrine (1 Cor. 14:6). These, in addition to deliverance, must be components of the diet of God's people.

A diet is defined as habitual nourishment. It is derived from the Greek word *diaita* meaning "manner of living." In other words, this is to be our manner of living.

No matter how many demons are cast out of a person's life, they will return unless the person lives their life in accordance with the

Word of God. We need to develop good spiritual habits when it comes to the Word and deliverance.

Prophetic ministry is also an important part of a believer's diet. Prophecy edifies, exhorts, and comforts (1 Cor. 14). The prophetic word builds up the saints. Just as natural foods build up the natural body, so prophecy builds up the spiritual man. Prophecy provides spiritual nourishment to the people of God. Prophecy is a part of "every word that proceeds from the mouth of God" (Matt. 4:4).

In conclusion, a proper diet for every child of God includes anointed preaching, teaching, prophetic ministry, personal Bible study, and deliverance. The result will be healthy, strong, and mature believers and strong local churches. We cannot afford to overemphasize one and deemphasize another. We need them all!

PRAYERS FOR DELIVERANCE

Keep my soul, and deliver me (Ps. 25:20).

Be pleased, O LORD, to deliver me (Ps. 40:13).

Make haste, O God, and deliver me (Ps. 70:1).

Deliver me in Your righteousness (Ps. 71:2).

Deliver me, O God, out of the hand of the enemy (Ps. 71:4).

Deliver me from my persecutors (Ps. 142:6).

Deliver me out of great waters (Ps. 144:7).

Deliver me from the oppression of man (Ps. 119:134).

Deliver me according to Your Word (Ps. 119:170).

Deliver my soul from lying lips and a deceitful tongue (Ps. 120:2).

Deliver me from my enemies and hide me (Ps. 143:9).

Surround me with songs of deliverance (Ps. 32:7).

Command deliverances for my life (Ps. 44:4).

Deliver me from all my fears (Ps. 34:4).

Deliver me out of all my trouble (Ps. 54:7).

Deliver me from them who hate me (Ps. 69:14).

Deliver me out of my distresses (Ps. 107:6).

Send Your Word and deliver me out of destruction (Ps. 107:20).

Deliver my soul from death, my eyes from tears, and my feet from falling (Ps. 116:8).

I call upon the name of Jesus, and I am delivered (Joel 2:32).

Deliver me from the power of the lion (Dan. 6:27).

Through Your knowledge I am delivered (Prov. 11:9).

Through Your wisdom I am delivered (Prov. 28:26).

I receive miracles of deliverance for my life (Dan. 6:27).

Prayers for Deliverance From Evil

Deliver me from evil (Matt. 6:13).

I pray that You would keep me from evil (1 Chron. 4:10).

No evil will touch me (Job 5:19).

Put to shame those who wish me evil (Ps. 40:14).

Let no evil disease cleave to my body (Ps. 41:8).

I will not be afraid of evil tidings (Ps. 112:7).

I will not be visited with evil (Prov. 19:23).

I refrain my feet from every evil way so that I might keep Your Word (Ps. 119:101).

Preserve me from all evil (Ps. 121:7).

Deliver me from the evil man (Ps. 140:1).

Let people be healed of plagues and evil spirits (Luke 7:21).

I pray that You would keep me from evil (John 17:15).

Let evil spirits be cast out (Acts 19:12).

I will not be overcome with evil, but I overcome evil with good (Rom. 12:21).

I put on the whole armor of God, that I might stand in the evil day (Eph. 6:13).

I cancel all the plans and forces of evil sent against my life.

Let the works of evil be burned by Your holy fire.

Let men repent of evil and turn to righteousness.

Let no evil be established in my life, but let Your righteousness be established.

I loose myself from all evildoers and evil soul ties.

CHAPTER 3
REJECTION: THE DOORWAY TO DEMONIC OPPRESSION

Having prayed for believers of many nations, I have come to this conclusion: the greatest undiagnosed, therefore, untreated malady in the body of Christ today is rejection. Rejection, whether active or passive, real or imaginary, robs Jesus Christ of His rightful lordship in the life of His children and robs them of the vitality and quality of life that Jesus intended.[1]

—NOEL AND PHYL GIBSON

GOD CREATED US to be loved. Every person needs love. You need the love of a family, the love of others, the love of a father—you need the love of God. You were created to be loved. And if you don't get that love, you will either accept rejection or will manifest fear or pride as the two manifestations of rejection. The enemy will use these two manifestations to open the door for demons to come into your life. The enemy knows how to destroy a person's life through rejection. Rejection is a door opener for all kinds of demonic oppression to come into a person's life.

HOW DO YOU GET A SPIRIT OF REJECTION?

Most people have suffered rejection early in life as a fetus in their mothers' wombs, through prenatal curses, being unwanted or illegitimate children, abandonment, birth order, adoption, or molestation.

A person can experience rejection before birth in a number of ways. They may receive a spirit of rejection because of the manner or timing of conception; for example, if the mother was raped or molested or was having an extramarital affair and got pregnant.

Children born under these circumstances may show a spirit of rejection. Also children born out of wedlock or to parents who did not want them, who are a strain on the family budget, the last of a large family, and the middle child of a family often struggle with rejection. The circumstances surrounding a pregnant woman and her attitude to her unborn child influences the child in the womb. The father's attitude toward an unborn child also has an impact. Some fathers want a son and end up having a girl. That child may receive a spirit of rejection and feel bad that she is displeasing to her father and wish that she was a boy instead. Same thing with boys whose parents wished they were girls.

How a child is born can also cause them to receive a spirit of rejection. If a child was born very quickly and was rushed out of the birth canal (via forceps or vacuum, for example), he or she may not have had time to transition to life outside the womb. Abrupt exposure to noise, bright lights, and physical handling after the warmth and security of the womb can be traumatic. A child who's born after long and protracted labor in which the mother and the baby have both become exhausted and a child born by Cesarean section may also develop a spirit of rejection.

A baby not bonded to its mother soon after birth may have a sense of being rejected. An adopted child is always a rejected child. Rejected parents produce rejected children. There is hereditary rejection. Parents who have suffered from hereditary rejection or who have been rejected before marriage will be unable to share personal warmth with their children. Without a doubt they love their children, but because they don't come from a family that expressed love or a close emotional bound, they are unable to express love physically. It is not uncommon to hear a parent say, "We are not a demonstrative family," or "We are not the kissing or hugging types." Translated this probably means, "We are embarrassed about any show of affection."

So the children grow up rejected, insecure, and lacking in self-worth despite being surrounded by materialistic replacements.

Other causes of rejection at the beginning of life

- Being born the gender opposite of what the parents wanted
- Being born with a deformity or physical disability
- Constant criticism by parents, siblings, or authority figures
- Unjust discipline, particularly if another family member appears to be favored
- Being called names that emphasize embarrassing personal features
- A sick or incapacitated brother or sister receiving prolonged medical care and attention
- Fathers showing weakness, apathy, or passivity in their authority or responsibility roles
- Subjection to sexual molestation or incest
- A father becoming sexually aggressive to his wife in the presence of his children
- A spoiled or pampered child will end up feeling rejected.
- Children who belong to a racial minority will usually feel rejected by the majority amongst whom they live and play.
- Speech difficulties such as stuttering, stammering, lisping, or an inability to pronounce certain consonants or words
- Unhappy parents who argue, fight, won't talk to each other, or only speak to their children—the children will feel guilty and responsible.
- Parental cruelty

- Alcoholism in one or both parents
- Failure to be forgiven or trusted by the parents
- Bribes or threats to be academically successful
- Being expelled from school or rejected by a peer group
- Embarrassed over the parents' religious beliefs
- A father showing more attention to his daughter's girl-friends than he does to his own daughter
- Destruction of the family home by fire or some natural disaster
- A family member convicted for a serious crime
- A sudden drop in the family's standard of living caused by the unemployment, redundancy, or bankruptcy of the breadwinner
- Parents who have ample financial resources but show meanness toward their children, causing them to feel ashamed before their playmates
- Children constantly being left to their own resources either because of the working hours of their parents or the disinterest in their children's welfare
- Parents showing no active interest in the progress of their children's schoolwork, sports activities, or leisure time pursuits

Causes of rejection later in life

- Being deserted or divorced by a mate
- The death or unfaithfulness of a marriage partner
- Mental or physical cruelty caused by a husband or wife
- Shame caused by a court conviction for a criminal offense
- The serving of a prison term

- Inability to find any long-term relief for mental, emotional, or physical problems after having exhausted all forms of counseling or professional services.
- Incompatible religious ideologies in marriage involving one partner being forced to comply with the other's wishes
- A lowering of lifestyle standards caused by the drinking habits of a marriage partner
- Rejection in love or a broken engagement
- Becoming bedridden or crippled as a result of disease or an accident
- Becoming subject to pressures beyond one's ability to control
- Being fired for incompetency, laid off, or being unable to find employment over a long period of time
- Being totally let down by people who had been trusted and whose advice had been totally relied upon
- Financial embarrassment caused by the failure of investments taken on by the advice of a close friend or being financially cheated by unscrupulous operators
- An over-fertile imagination, particularly if indulging in self-pity

Cultural or ethnic rejection

Another form of rejection is rejection because of a person's cultural background or ethnicity. There are strongholds in this form of rejection that are just in the bloodline. You don't have to do anything wrong to be rejected by people. The color of your skin can cause rejection, but it opens you up to so many demons, and Jesus wants to deliver you from this. We can see that this kind of rejection goes back to the Bible.

> ...lest there be any fornicator or profane person like Esau, who for one morsel of food sold his birthright. For you know that afterward, when he wanted to inherit the blessing, *he was rejected*, for he found no place for repentance, though he sought it diligently with tears.
>
> —HEBREWS 12:16–17, EMPHASIS ADDED

Esau was rejected, and as a result many of his people, the Edomites, carried a spirit of rejection.

Same thing with Ishmaelites—the descendants of Ishmael, who today are known as the Arabic people of the world, carry a strong spirit of rejection. And the Jewish people of the world carry a strong spirit of rejection. When you come to Christ and you are an Arabic or Jewish believer, you will need deliverance. Many African Americans need deliverance because of societal rejection, racism, and prejudice. So it's not a black or a white thing, a Jewish thing or an Arabic thing. God is no respecter of persons. It's the history of certain people. American Indians in this country who have suffered from so much rejection need major deliverance when they come to Christ.

If you have a familial, racial, or cultural history that is one filled with rejection, you will need to deal with these roots of rejection to be set free so you can prosper and be blessed and not operate in pride, fear, sickness, poverty, witchcraft, religion, legalism, and all the other demons that come in because of rejection.

WHAT ARE THE SIGNS AND SYMPTOMS OF A SPIRIT OF REJECTION?

Schizophrenia begins with rejection, opens the door for a split personality, making a person double minded. Here are some signs and symptoms that a person may have a spirit of rejection:

- A constant desire for physical love and assurance of self-worth
- Addiction
- Attention-seeking
- Despair
- Despondency
- Discouragement
- Envy
- Fantasy
- Fears
- Frustration
- Guilt
- Hopelessness
- Impatience
- Inferiority
- Inordinate affection for animals
- Loneliness
- Lust
- Perverseness
- Pride
- Revenge
- Self-rejection
- Sensitivity
- Shame
- Suicide
- Unworthiness
- Vanity
- Withdrawal

REJECTED BY GOD?

Being rejected by God comes as a result of a person refusing the knowledge of God (Hosea 4:6). I have heard people say God doesn't reject anyone. Let me first say this: God is a God of love. Anyone who repents and comes to God in faith He will never reject. He says, "Come to Me, all you who labor and are heavy laden, and I will give you rest" (Matt. 11:28). God encourages people. He is no respecter of persons. He doesn't reject people based on their color, culture, or gender. God is love: "The one who comes to Me I will by no means cast out" (John 6:37). So God will never reject anyone who comes to Him in faith, love, and repentance. But that does not mean that God does not reject people.

Throughout the Bible we see that God rejects certain people. Adam was the first person to be rejected. He was put out of the garden and rejected by God for his disobedience. (See Genesis 3.) Cain's offering was rejected by God, and he murdered his brother, Abel (Gen. 4:3–10). Ishmael was rejected by God (Gen. 21:8–21). Although God loved him and promised to bless his generations as well, he still suffered rejection by God all because of Abraham and Sarah's impatience. Abraham and Sarah couldn't wait for the promise of God to be fulfilled in their lives. They tried to help God by using Sarah's maid, Hagar, as a surrogate. (See Genesis 16:1–4.) This caused Ishmael to be rejected by God as Abraham's promised seed.

Saul was another one who was rejected by God. He was from the smallest tribe in Israel, the tribe of Benjamin, and the smallest family in that tribe. Before God rejected him, he already had a spirit of self-rejection, inferiority, and insecurity (1 Samuel 15:17 says, "When you were little in your own eyes, were you not head of the tribes of Israel?"). Becoming the first king of Israel caused these strongholds to manifest even more. When he was anointed king of Israel he manifested rebellion and disobedience. He went out to battle one time and chose to do things his own way, and immediately, because of his arrogance, impatience, and lack of submission to the prophet of God, he was rejected as king of Israel.

> Behold, to obey is better than sacrifice,
> And to heed than the fat of rams.
> For rebellion is as the sin of witchcraft,
> And stubbornness is as iniquity and idolatry.
> Because you have rejected the word of the LORD,
> He also has rejected you from being king.
> —1 SAMUEL 15:22–23

After this rejection the door opened for all kinds of demons to oppress Saul. He began to manifest paranoia, suspicion, a murderous spirit, witchcraft, and finally suicide. This is a picture of how demons can destroy a person through rejection.

It was not God who first rejected Saul. Saul rejected God through disobedience and determination to go against what he knew the Lord had commanded him to do. Saul's life was destroyed by this demon of rejection. It sent him on a collision course. His whole life went downhill. It was all a result of the demon of rejection.

> My people are destroyed for lack of knowledge.
> Because you have rejected knowledge,
> I also will reject you from being priest for Me;
> Because you have forgotten the law of your God,
> I also will forget your children.
> —HOSEA 4:6

This is a curse of rejection. But there is deliverance, and there is forgiveness. If a person repents and says, "I want the knowledge of God. I want to seek God. I want to know His Word," that person can be delivered from rejection.

But I'm here to tell you that if you reject deliverance, if you reject the knowledge of the Word, the knowledge of the prophetic, and say, "I don't want it," God will reject you. There are some people groups who don't know certain things because they have never been presented with them. But we can hardly say that in America. Here, in some way or another, we have been presented with truth, deliverance, healing, the prophetic, and the apostolic. Well, God says, "If you reject knowledge, I will reject you."

When you are rejected by God, that opens the door to the spirit of rejection. When that root of rejection comes into your life, it will open the door to a host of other demons to come in that will destroy your life. God says, "My people are destroyed for lack of knowledge."

The spirit of destruction is the result of being rejected by God. When this happens, whole groups of people, whole families can be rejected and end up being destroyed and devastated by the enemy. This is why it is so important to repent and accept the truth of God when the Spirit of God is dealing with you. There is no need to take any chances at being reprobate like the people mentioned in Romans 1:26–32. I encourage you to open your Bible and read that passage now.

There's this whole issue today of whether or not homosexuals or lesbians can be married. That fact is God rejects it. God will never accept a marriage between two men or two women. It is rejected by God. When something is rejected by God, it cannot be blessed. It always comes under a curse.

In our society today people are pushing the homosexual lifestyle and other perverse lifestyles so much until many of them have crossed the line. They have rejected the Word of God. They have rejected God's plan for family and marriage to the extent that they are in danger of being rejected by God. That is a dangerous condition to be in.

I would warn you that if you are a part of a community that

is promoting a homosexual lifestyle and you reject the Bible, Christianity, God, and His design of marriage between a man and a woman, you reject truth, and you will get into a place where you end up being reprobate, completely demonized, and destroyed by the enemy.

The word *reprobate* means worthless, cast away, rejected—like garbage, trash. This is a person whose very mind has been rejected by God.

In Romans 1:29–31 there is a list of demons that come in as a result of being given over to a reprobate mind. They are all names of evil spirits that come into individuals' lives who have been rejected by God: "unrighteousness, sexual immorality, wickedness, covetousness, maliciousness; full of envy, murder, strife, deceit, evil-mindedness; they are whisperers, backbiters, haters of God, violent, proud, boasters, inventors of evil things, disobedient to parents, undiscerning, untrustworthy, unloving, unforgiving, unmerciful." If you continue in sin and reject God, you can come to a place where God rejects you and you are given over to spirit of destruction.

I know you may not hear this in churches today, but the Bible shows that God rejected Cain, Saul, and even the children of Israel because they disobeyed His commandments. He rejected them, put them out of the land, and sent them to Babylon. (See Genesis 4:5; 1 Samuel 16:1; Hosea 1:10.) He rejected the priesthood of Eli, because Eli would not correct his sons. (See 1 Samuel 2:12–4:18.) Eli was rejected and the priesthood was taken from him. God rejected Esau and chose Jacob. He rejected Ishmael and chose Isaac. God does not accept anything but that which is worthy of Him accepting. He doesn't accept any kind of sacrifice, any kind of offering, or any kind of lifestyle. And there is a real danger of being rejected.

But rejection by God or any other kind of rejection is not the will of God for you. You can repent today, accept Jesus, and be delivered from any demons and spirits whether they are lust, rejection, hatred, anger, bitterness, or resentment that may be operating in your life. God loves you and wants to save and deliver you. Call out to Him, and He will answer you.

WHAT FREES YOU FROM A SPIRIT OF REJECTION?

The Bible says, "Whom the Son sets free is free indeed" (John 8:36). Through Jesus we have been set free from every demon in hindrance and attack from the enemy. His Word shows us the way to freedom from a spirit of rejection to a life lived under the revelation that we are accepted in the Beloved. Let's look at how we can be set free by the truth in God's Word.

Knowledge, light, and revelation

A verse in Proverbs says, "Through knowledge the righteous will be delivered" (Prov. 11:9). Knowledge can literally deliver you. Demons do not want you to have any knowledge of deliverance or the realm of how they operate because they are creatures of darkness: "For we do not wrestle against flesh and blood, but against principalities, against powers, against the *rulers of the darkness*" (Eph. 6:12, emphasis added). Satan can only rule where there is darkness or ignorance. So light and revelation brought about through knowledge always exposes and breaks the power of the rulers of darkness in your life.

There is such a lack of teaching and revelation in the local churches. People who receive teaching and revelation of deliverance will not only receive deliverance for their own lives but will also be better equipped to minister deliverance to the lives of others. I hope to give you some basic knowledge in this book that I believe will set you free from the oppression of the enemy.

Revelation of the rejection of Christ

Jesus was rejected so that you could be delivered from rejection. Isaiah 53:3 tells us that He was despised and rejected of men. He was rejected by the high priests and the Pharisees. Why did Jesus go through rejection as one of the major areas in His passion? Because man needs to be delivered from rejection. He took upon Himself our rejection so that He could deliver us from rejection. The biggest rejection came when He said, "My God, My God, why have You forsaken Me" (Matt. 27:46), because at that moment He became sin, and His Father rejected Him. God always rejects sin. Jesus became sin, went through rejection, suffered, and was beaten, wounded, and bruised in order to deliver us from rejection.

Rejection is a major stronghold and a major aspect of deliverance and salvation. And now because of Christ's rejection, we can be accepted in the Beloved. We can be accepted through the blood of Jesus. We can be accepted by grace. We don't have to be perfected through legalism or keeping laws. We can be accepted by faith.

> He chose us in Him before the foundation of the world, that we should be holy and without blame before Him in love, having predestined us to adoption as sons by Jesus Christ to Himself, according to the good pleasure of His will, to the praise of the glory of His grace, by which *He has made us accepted in the Beloved.*
> —Ephesians 1:4–6, emphasis added

This is the tremendous blessing of Christianity, and it is the only religion that teaches salvation by grace. Every other religion teaches salvation by works, that somehow you have to earn God's favor. No, our salvation is by grace and faith. Jesus earned it for us. We can receive it by faith. That is why accepting Christ is the only way to God. It is the only basis of salvation. Every other religion is false and rooted in deception, and people are bound because of rejection. Rejection always opens the door for you to perform your way into being accepted by God.

What do Muslims do? They have to pray five times a day and go to Mecca. They have to do this and that, always performing, always trying to earn God's love. What is the root of many Arabic people who are the majority of Muslims? Ishmael. They are Ishmaelites. What did Ishmael suffer from? Rejection. That root of rejection has opened up an entire culture to being deceived into thinking they can earn their way into heaven. The good news is that there is deliverance through Jesus Christ.

Look at the Indian people—their caste system is loaded with rejection. Hinduism is about being in the right caste. If you're in the low caste, you're rejected. They are taught that if they do what is good in this life, they may be able to come back as something better in the next life. So there is always a performance orientation in their culture. They work at being perfect, and they work at being accepted.

That's what rejected people do: they work and work and work for society or for others to accept them. The truth is you can only be accepted by grace, faith, and mercy. You need to get delivered from any spirits that try to make you perform up to the level of society or other people to make you accepted. Now that doesn't mean that you shouldn't do right to be accepted, but it simply means that the desire to be accepted should not drive you and dominate your life. If it does, then it's demonic.

Prayer

Prayer is a most powerful weapon in the fight against rejection. Prayer brings you into the presence of God. Prayer opens up your spirit to hear the truth of your acceptance through Christ. Prayer builds up your inner man.

Psalm 144:1 is a prayer you should consistently pray over your life, so that you will be able to fight against spiritual opposition that comes against your life. It says, "Blessed be the LORD my Rock, who trains my hands for war, and my fingers for battle." God will give you the strategy to gain victory over rejection.

Psalm 18 is one of the most inspirational psalms when it comes to spiritual warfare. Praying some of the key verses in this chapter will build your faith to see great deliverance in your life. For example, verse 19 says that deliverance brings us into a large or broad place. Sometimes the enemy wants to confine, restrict, and limit us. But through spiritual warfare we can break the limitations. We can ask God to deliver us from demons that block and obstruct our way so that we can come into a larger place. Rejection is one of these kind of demons that make it hard for us to move to the next level in our lives. But the Lord has given you the necks of your enemies, and you will destroy them in His name (v. 40).

Second Samuel 19:3 is another scripture we pray during deliverance ministry at our church because sometimes the enemy tries to bring rejection into our lives by stealth, or when we are not aware and it's undetected. A stealth bomber goes under the radar. The radar cannot pick up a stealth bomber. The military developed stealth technology so that they could enter a region undetected and do damage. And so I encourage people to pray 2 Samuel 19:3 to bind and expose and cast out the rejection demon that would try by stealth or undetection to come into their lives. This verse works against any demonic spirit that tries to sneak into your life undetected.

The anointing of God

Psalm 18:50 says, "Great deliverance He gives to His king, and shows mercy to His anointed." If you are saved and baptized in the Holy Spirit, you are God's anointed. You are anointed by God, and when the enemy attacks God's anointed, God wants to give you great deliverance. You can pray, "I am Your anointed, and You give me great deliverance over the spirit of rejection." He will do it; He will show mercy to you and give you victory over it.

Perseverance

> I have pursued my enemies and overtaken them; neither
> did I turn back again till they were destroyed.
>
> —PSALM 18:37

This is perseverance. This is being a person who is persistent in warfare. Do not stop until the spirit is gone, whether it's witchcraft, sickness, poverty, or rejection. Whatever is attacking your life, do not retreat until it is completely annihilated by the power of God.

Your spiritual authority

One of the most important principles of spiritual warfare is that you must use your authority against the enemy. Jesus said, "I give unto *you* power [*power* is the Greek word *exousia*, which means 'authority'] to tread upon serpents and scorpions, and over all the power of the enemy: and nothing shall by any means hurt you" (Luke 10:19, KJV, emphasis added). Now some people say you can't be hurt by the enemy, because Jesus says, "I give you power." But that's only if you *use* the authority. Just because you have been given authority doesn't mean you've used it. If you don't exercise your authority, you cannot claim the second part of that verse, "nothing shall by any means hurt you." We must exercise our authority, and one of the ways we do that is through prayer, through binding and loosing, and through commands and decrees that we release through our words. So it's important to exercise your authority over the enemy on a consistent basis.

Remember the story of the Gatherene demoniac in Matthew chapter 8? There were two of them in the account. The Bible says that they blocked the road. Those two demonized men would not let anyone pass that way. It is a picture of how demons will try to block your way. You need to bind and rebuke any demon that will try to block your path or your way in the name of Jesus.

Psalm 91:13 says, "You shall tread upon the lion and the cobra, the young lion and the serpent you shall trample underfoot." The enemy is under your feet. That represents total authority and victory. Make this your confession and go forth in victory and in the power of God.

Rejection Must Go!

We must be able to identify the causes of rejection and be able to come against the demons of rejection, fear of rejection, self-rejection, hereditary rejection, roots of rejection, and the spirits that come in with rejection: hurt, anger, bitterness, rage, pride, fear, rebellion, and more. All of these things can torment your life. Jesus does not want you to be tormented. He wants you to be set free. You are not alone. So many people need deliverance from these demons of rejection and the other demons that accompany the demons of rejection. God wants to set us all free from the spirit of rejection so that we can bring deliverance to our families and friends and those around us. Jesus said, "The Spirit of the Lord is upon me, because he hath anointed me to preach the gospel to the poor; he hath sent me to heal the brokenhearted, to preach deliverance to the captives" (Luke 4:18, kjv). He imparted this responsibility on us as well.

But you must minister deliverance to yourself first. Jesus talked about this when He said, "First remove the plank from your own eye, and then you will see clearly to remove the speck out of your brother's eye" (Matt. 7:5). That phrase *cast out* carries the same meaning when the Bible speaks, in other passages, of casting out demons. It is the Greek word *ekballō*. It means to expel or eject.[2] So there are things we need to drive out of our own lives before we can successfully minister to other people. We will talk about this more in the next chapter.

Prayers for Deliverance From Rejection

I declare that You have sanctified me with Your Word; Your Word over me is truth (John 17:17).

Lord, You are my light and my salvation. You are the strength of my life. I will not fear anything or anyone (Ps. 27:1).

I believe and receive what You have said about me.

Your truth sets me free from a spirit of rejection.

You have nailed my rejection to the cross. I am set free.

You were despised and rejected. You are acquainted with my grief and sorrow. But by Your stripes, I am healed of rejection (Isa. 53:3–5).

The Lord is with me. I will not be afraid. What can man do to me? (Ps. 118:6).

The lines have fallen to me in pleasant places; yes, I have a good inheritance (Ps 16:6).

I am blessed with all spiritual blessings in heavenly places in Christ (Eph. 1:3).

I have been chosen by God from the foundation of the world (Eph. 1:4).

I am holy and without blame (Eph. 1:4).

I have been adopted as Your child according to the good pleasure of Your will (Eph. 1:5).

I am accepted in the Beloved (Eph. 1:6).

I am redeemed through the blood of Jesus (Eph. 1:7).

I am an heir (Eph. 1:11).

I am seated in heavenly places in Christ Jesus (Eph. 2:6).

I am the workmanship of the Lord, created in Christ Jesus for good works (Eph. 2:10).

I am a fellow citizen with the saints and members of the household of God (Eph. 2:19).

I have been given exceedingly great and precious promises, that I may be a partaker of the divine nature of Christ (2 Pet. 1:4).

My inner man is strengthened with might by the Spirit of God (Eph. 3:16).

I am rooted and grounded in love (Eph. 3:17).

I am renewed in the spirit of my mind (Eph. 4:23).

I walk in love (Eph. 5:2).

I am filled with the Spirit of God (Eph. 5:18).

I am more than a conqueror (Rom. 8:37).

I am an overcomer by the blood of the Lamb (Rev. 12:11).

I am the righteousness of God in Christ Jesus (2 Cor. 5:21).

I am healed (1 Pet. 2:24).

The Son has set me free (John 8:36).

I am born of God, therefore I am victorious (1 John 5:4).

CHAPTER 4
"LOOSE THYSELF"
—SELF-DELIVERANCE

Shake thyself from the dust; arise, and sit down, O Jerusalem: loose
thyself *from the bands of thy neck, O captive daughter of Zion.*

—ISAIAH 52:2, KJV, EMPHASIS ADDED

T HIS IS A prophetic word to the church that says, "Loose thyself!" It is a powerful verse that relates to self-deliverance. We
have been given the power and authority to loose ourselves
from all types of bondage.

Synonyms for the word *loose* include: disjoin, divorce, separate,
asunder, sever, unhitch, disconnect, detach, unseat, unbind, unchain,
unfetter, unloose, free, release, liberate, break up, break in pieces,
smash, shatter, splinter, demolish, cleave, force apart. It also means
to forgive or pardon.

"Zion" is a prophetic word and symbol for the church. Isaiah
prophesied that Zion would be a "captive daughter." This is so true
of the condition of the church today. Even though many are saved
and have received the promise of the Spirit, there are still many
bondages that remain in the lives of believers.

SELF-DELIVERANCE

The question is often asked of me, "Can a person deliver himself of
demons?" My answer is yes. It is also my conviction that a person
cannot really keep himself free of demons until he is walking in this
dominion of deliverance.

How is it that a person can deliver himself? As a believer (and that
is our assumption), a person has the same authority as the believer
who is ministering deliverance to another. He has the authority in

49

the name of Jesus, and Jesus plainly promised them that believe: "In my name shall they cast out devils" (Mark 16:17, KJV).

Usually a person needs only to learn how to go about self-deliverance. After a person has experienced an initial deliverance at the hands of an experienced minister, he can begin to practice self-deliverance.[1] The good news is that we have been given a prophetic promise and a command to loose ourselves. Jesus told His disciples that "whatsoever" we loosed on earth is loosed in heaven (Matt. 18:18, KJV).

In the ensuing pages we will examine the "whatsoever." In other words, whatsoever is binding, harassing, or operating in your life, contrary to the will of God, can be loosed from your life because you have been given the authority to do so.

The range of things that can bind a believer is almost limitless. There are many bondages we can categorize that need to be exposed and broken in the lives of all believers. Once you identify the enemy, you can then proceed to free yourself from his clutches.

LOOSE THYSELF FROM THE PAST

I have ministered to many believers who are still bound and tied to their past. The past can be a chain that keeps you from enjoying the present and being successful in the future.

While ministering deliverance to a young man, I encountered a strong spirit dwelling in him who boasted that he would not depart. I commanded the spirit to identify himself, and he replied that his name was Past.

The spirit proceeded to explain that it was his job to keep the young man bound to his past so that he could not be successful in his Christian walk. The young man had been through a divorce, and his past continued to haunt him.

This encounter helped to give me a revelation of the fact that there are numerous spirits assigned to people to keep them bound to the past that has left scars and wounds that have not completely healed. Many of these wounds have been infected and have become the dwelling places of unclean spirits.

People need to be loosed not only from demons but also from other people. Ungodly soul ties are avenues through which spirits of control and manipulation utilize when working upon their unwary victims.

Let's look at some of the things that could cause spirits to attach themselves to people who have had traumatic experiences in their past. For the purposes of clarity, we find the word *trauma* defined by Webster's as "a disordered psychic or behavioral state resulting from severe mental or emotional stress or physical injury."[2]

Traumatic experiences can open the door for demons. These can and often include accidents. Mentioned below are two such traumatic experiences that greatly affect the lives of individuals.

1. Rape

> They have raped the women in Zion, the virgins in the towns of Judah.
>
> —LAMENTATIONS 5:11, JB

Rape is one of the most traumatic experiences a person can have. It is a violation that leaves deep scares in the psyche of the person who is victimized by this ungodly act. The door is opened for a host of evil spirits to enter and operate throughout the life of the victim.

Spirits of hurt, distrust, lust, perversion, anger, hatred, rage, bitterness, shame, guilt, and fear can enter and torment the person for the rest of their life if not discerned and cast out. Rape can also be a curse, and there is often a history of this sin in the bloodline.

Rape has always been in the history of oppressed people. It was (and is) common for victors to rape the women of the vanquished. It is one of the most shameful and humiliating acts that can be perpetrated upon an oppressed people.

Often victims of rape carry sexual blockages into marriage, including spirits of frigidity, bound and blocked emotions, hatred of men, and fear of sexual intercourse. Individuals can grow up with deep roots of bitterness that poison the system, opening the door for spirits of sickness and infirmity, including cancer.

> *Father, in Jesus's name, I loose myself from this prowling demon that sought to steal, kill, and destroy my body, my sexuality, and my worth. I loose myself from any hatred, bitterness, and unforgiveness. I loose myself from blaming myself for this violation. I loose myself from any soul ties, spirits of infirmity, or other evil spirits that would seek to latch on to my life because of this trauma. I loose myself from any bondages that would keep me from experiencing healthy and free marital intimacy. Amen.*

2. Incest

Another common sexual violation is the sin of incest. Incest can also result from a curse, and there can be a history of this sin in the bloodline. It is an act that causes much shame and guilt. It opens the door for all kinds of curses, including insanity, death, destruction, confusion, perversion, and sickness. Often the victim blames himself for this act even though it may have been the result of a seducing spirit.

> *Father, in Jesus's name, I loose myself from the shame, guilt, soul ties, and any other hindering spirit that would try to keep me from living a whole and healthy life. I loose myself from the painful memories of this abuse and declare that I am washed clean, inside and out. I loose myself from every demonic spirit that would seek to enter through this open door, and I shut this*

> *door to my past and pray a hedge of protection around*
> *my future. Amen.*

LOOSE THYSELF FROM UNGODLY SOUL TIES

Cursed be their anger, for it was fierce; and their wrath, for it was cruel: I will divide them in Jacob, and scatter them in Israel.

—GENESIS 49:7

The Lord separated Simeon and Levi because they exerted a bad influence upon one another. A soul tie is a bond between two individuals; the souls (minds, wills, emotions) of individuals knit or joined together. Ungodly soul ties can be formed through fornication (Gen. 34:2–3) and witchcraft (Gal. 3:1; 4:17).

As mentioned earlier, people need to be loosed not only from demons but also from other people. Ungodly soul ties are avenues through which spirits of control, domination, witchcraft, and manipulation operate. If you are linked with the wrong people, you will be in bondage, often unknowingly.

It is never the will of God for one individual to control another. True freedom is being delivered from any controlling power that hinders you from fulfilling the will of God. Often those under control are unaware that they are being controlled. This is why many times the control is so difficult to break.

An ungodly soul tie will result in the presence of an evil influence in your life. While good soul ties help you in your walk with God, ungodly soul ties hinder you in your walk with the Lord.

Ungodly soul ties in the Bible include: 1) Ahab and Jezebel (1 Kings 18); 2) Solomon and his wives—they turned his heart away from the Lord (1 Kings 11:1–4); and 3) Levi and Simeon (Gen. 49:5–7).

Father, in Jesus's name, I loose myself from all relationships that are not ordained of God, all relationships that are not of the Spirit but of the flesh, all relationship based on control, domination, or manipulation, and all relationships based on lust and deception. Amen.

LOOSE YOUR MEMORY

Forgetting those things which are behind...
—PHILIPPIANS 3:13

There is an evil spirit named memory recall that can cause a person to have flashbacks of past experiences. This keeps a person in bondage to traumatic experiences of the past. This spirit causes a person to remember experiences of hurt, pain, and rejection. Although there may be experiences in your life you will never completely forget, you should not be in bondage to the past through your memory.

The enemy should not be able to trigger things in your memory that hinder you in your present or future life. This is why your memory needs to be loosed from bad experiences of hurt and trauma.

Father, in Jesus's name, I loose myself from the effects of all the bad memories, painful memories, and memories of the past that would hinder me in the present or future. Amen.

LOOSE THYSELF FROM UNFORGIVENESS AND BITTERNESS

Unforgiveness opens the door for tormenting spirits (Matt. 18). Bitterness opens the door for spirits of infirmity, including arthritis and cancer. It is symbolized by gall and wormwood. Unforgiveness is the result of being hurt, rejected, abandoned, disappointed, abused, raped, molested, taken advantage of, lied on, cheated, talked about, etc.

Father, in Jesus's name, I loose myself from all bitterness,
unforgiveness, and resentment. I loose to God those who
have offended me or hurt me in anyway. I loose myself
from all spirits of infirmity as a result of my bitterness.
I close that door, in Jesus's name. Amen.

LOOSE YOUR EMOTIONS

Are you loosed in your emotions? The emotions are a part of the soul along with the will and the mind. There are many people bound and blocked in their emotions. Spirits of hurt, rejection, anger, broken heart, grief, sadness, hatred, bitterness, and rage can occupy the emotions, causing emotional pain.

Your emotions were created by God to express joy and sorrow. Both should be natural responses to different situations. The enemy, however, comes in to cause extremes in the emotional realm and even blockage whereby a person is unable to express the proper emotions.

Emotional pain and bondage can come as a result of traumatic experiences of the past, including rape, incest, abuse, death of a loved one, war, tragedies, rejection, abandonment, accidents, etc.

In the name of the Lord Jesus Christ, by the authority
given to me to bind and loose, I loose my emotions from
every evil spirit that has come in as a result of experi-
ences of the past. I loose myself from all hurt, deep hurt,
pain, sadness, grief, anger, hatred, rage, bitterness, fear,
and bound and blocked emotions. I command these
spirits to come out, and I decree freedom to my emo-
tions in the name of the Lord Jesus Christ. Amen.

LOOSE THYSELF FROM OCCULT BONDAGE

The word *occult* means hidden. Involvement in the occult opens the door for many demons, including spirits of depression, suicide, death, destruction, sickness, mental illness, addiction, lust, etc. Occult practices include:

- Ouija board
- Horoscopes
- Palm reading
- Tea leaf reading
- Psychic
- Readers and advisers
- Drugs (from Greek word *pharmakeia—sorcery*)
- Black magic
- White magic
- ESP

> *Father, in Jesus's name, I loose myself from all occult involvement, all sorcery, divination, witchcraft, psychic inheritance, rebellion, all confusion, sickness, death, and destruction as a result of occult involvement. Amen.*

LOOSE YOUR MIND

For as he thinketh in his heart so is he.
—PROVERBS 23:7, KJV

You are the way you think. The mind has always been a favorite target of the enemy. If the devil can control your mind, he can control your life. Spirits that attack the mind include mind control, confusion, mental breakdown, mind-binding and mind-binding spirits, insanity, madness, mania, fantasy, evil thinking, migraines, mental pain, and negative thinking. They are all what I call "stinking thinking."

The good news is that you can loose yourself (including your mind) from all evil influences that operate through your mind.

Mind control is a common spirit that has been identified by the name Octopus. Mind control spirits can resemble an octopus or squid with tentacles that grasp and control the mind. Deliverance from mind control releases a person from mental pressure, mental pain, confusion, and mental torment. Mind control spirits can enter through listening to ungodly music, reading occult books, pornography, false teaching, false religions, drugs, and passivity.

> *In Jesus's name, I loose my mind from all spirits of control, confusion, mental bondage, insanity, madness, fantasy, passivity, intellectualism, knowledge block, ignorance, mind binding, lust, and evil thinking. Amen.*

LOOSE YOUR WILL

Not my will, but thine, be done.

—LUKE 22:42, KJV

One of the greatest gifts given to man is that of a *free will*. The freedom to choose and to decide is given to everyone. The Lord does not force us to obey Him. He gives us the choice to humble ourselves and submit our will to His will.

The devil, on the other hand, attempts to dominate and control our will for his evil purposes. When you find yourself unable to submit your will to the will of God, it is because your will is being controlled by the powers of darkness.

Your will needs to be *loosed* to follow the will of the Lord. Spirits that invade and control the will include stubbornness, self-will, anti-submissiveness, rebellion, pride, disobedience, lust and witchcraft.

> *Father, in Jesus's name, I loose my will from all control, domination, and manipulation from Satan, his demons, and other people. I loose my will from all lust, rebellion, stubbornness, pride, self-will, selfishness, and anti-submissive spirits that block and hinder my will. I*

break and loose myself from all chains around my will,
and I submit my will to the will of God. Amen.

Loose Your Sexual Character

Flee fornication.

—1 Corinthians 6:18, kjv

Lust is a spirit that is pervasive in our day and age. Sexual perversion includes incest, homosexuality, masturbation, pornography, fornication, and adultery.

The sex drive is one of the strongest appetites in the human body. Satan desires to control and pervert it outside the marital relationship in which it is blessed. Many believers struggle in this area with the companion spirits of guilt and condemnation.

Spirits of lust and perversion can operate in any part of the physical body, including the genitals, hands, eyes, mouth, stomach, and so on. Any part of the body given to sexual sin will be invaded and controlled by spirits of lust. (An example would be the eyes in viewing pornography, the hands in acts of masturbation, or the tongue in filthy conversation.)

> *In the name of Jesus, I loose all members of my body—*
> *including my mind, memory, eyes, ears, tongue, hands,*
> *feet, and my entire sexual character—from all lust,*
> *perversion, sexual impurity, uncleanness, lasciviousness,*
> *promiscuity, pornography, fornication, homosexuality,*
> *fantasy, filthiness, burning passion, and uncontrollable*
> *sex drive. Amen.*

Loose Thyself From Evil Inheritance

Weaknesses and tendencies can be inherited from the sins of the fathers. For example, a person born to alcoholic parents will have a higher chance of becoming an alcoholic. Sicknesses and diseases can run in the bloodline, which is why doctors will often check to see is there is a history of certain sicknesses in the family. Some of these evil inheritances include lust, perversion, witchcraft, pride, rebellion, divorce, alcohol, hatred, bitterness, idolatry, poverty, ignorance, and sicknesses (including heart disease, cancer, diabetes, and high blood pressure).

Familiar spirits are demons familiar with a person and the family because often they have been in the family for generations. Sometimes these spirits are difficult to break because of how deep their roots run into the family line. I'll talk more about how to break generational demons in the chapter on stubborn demons.

> *In the name of Jesus, I loose myself from all evil inheritance, including inherited weaknesses, attitudes, thought patterns, sickness, witchcraft, lust, rebellion, poverty, ungodly lifestyles, and strife. Amen.*

LOOSE THYSELF FROM FEAR

Fear is a paralyzing spirit that keeps people bound in many areas of their lives. This spirit manifests itself in numerous ways: fear of rejection (works with rejection and self-rejection), fear of hurt, fear of authority (including pastors), fear of witchcraft, fear of career, fear of dying, fear of failure, fear of the future, fear of responsibility, fear of darkness, fear of being alone, fear of what people think of you, fear of what people say about you, fear of hell, fear of demons and deliverance, fear of poverty, terror, fright, sudden fear, apprehension. All of these manifestations must be broken in the name of Jesus.

> *In the name of Jesus, I loose myself from all fears including childhood fears, fears from trauma, fears from the past, and all inherited fears. Amen.*

Loose Thyself From Rejection

Rejection prevents one from giving or receiving love from God or from other people. There is also a spirit called *rejection from the womb* that enters the womb because the child was unwanted.

Self-rejection and fear of rejection are other related spirits. Rejection is also a doorkeeper. This spirit opens the door for other spirits to enter, including fear, hurt, unforgiveness, and bitterness. It links with rebellion, causing schizophrenia.

Almost everyone has experienced rejection at one time or another in life. People can be rejected because of their gender, skin color, economic status, size, shape, etc. Rejection is a major stronghold in the lives of many.

> *In the name of Jesus, I loose myself from the spirit of rejection. I am accepted in the Beloved. I am the chosen one of God in Christ Jesus. I loose myself from self-rejection and sabotage. I loose myself from fear of man and people-pleasing. I seek only to please God. I loose myself to receive love from God and from others without fear. I close the door on rejection, fear, hurt, unforgiveness, bitterness, and rebellion. In Jesus's name, I pray. Amen.*

Loose Your Conscience

To be *loosed* means to be forgiven and pardoned. You have been forgiven by the Father through the blood of Jesus. You are loosed from guilt, shame, and condemnation. You must also be loosed from the law (legalism).

The law brings condemnation and judgment, but Jesus brings forgiveness and reconciliation. We loose our conscience by applying *the blood of Jesus,* by faith. Satan uses guilt and condemnation to beat down the believers. Believers who don't understand grace arc struggling in their Christian lives, never measuring up to religious standards imposed upon them through legalism. To be free in your conscience is to have peace in your mind. The peace of God rules in your heart.

> *In the name of Jesus, I loose myself from all guilt, shame, condemnation, self-condemnation, and legalism. Amen.*

PRAYERS FOR SELF-DELIVERANCE

I break all generational curses of pride, rebellion, lust, poverty, witchcraft, idolatry, death, destruction, failure, sickness, infirmity, fear, schizophrenia, and rejection in the name of Jesus.

I command all generational and hereditary spirits operating in my life through curses to be bound and cast out in the name of Jesus.

I command all spirits of lust, perversion, adultery, fornication, uncleanness, and immorality to come out of my sexual character in the name of Jesus.

I command all spirits of hurt, rejection, fear, anger, wrath, sadness, depression, discouragement, grief, bitterness, and unforgiveness to come out of my emotions in the name of Jesus.

I command all spirits of confusion, forgetfulness, mind control, mental illness, double-mindedness, fantasy, pain, pride, and memory recall to come out of my mind in the name of Jesus.

I break all curses of schizophrenia and command all spirits of double-mindedness, rejection, rebellion, and root of bitterness to come out in the name of Jesus.

I command all spirits of guilt, shame, and condemnation to come out of my conscience in the name of Jesus.

I command all spirits of pride, stubbornness, disobedience, rebellion, self-will, selfishness, and arrogance to come out of my will in the name of Jesus.

I command all spirits of addiction to come out of my appetite in the name of Jesus.

I command all spirits of witchcraft, sorcery, divination, and occult to come out in the name of Jesus.

I command all spirits operating in my head, eyes, mouth, tongue, and throat to come out in the name of Jesus.

I command all spirits operating in my chest and lungs to come out in the name of Jesus.

I command all spirits operating in my back and spine to come out in the name of Jesus.

I command all spirits operating in my stomach, navel, and abdomen to come out in the name of Jesus.

I command all spirits operating in my heart, spleen, kidneys, liver, and pancreas to come out in the name of Jesus.

I command all spirits operating in my sexual organs to come out in the name of Jesus.

I command all spirits operating in my hands, arms, legs, and feet to come out in the name of Jesus.

I command all demons operating in my skeletal system, including my bones, joints, knees, and elbows, to come out in the name of Jesus.

I command all spirits operating in my glands and endocrine system to come out in the name of Jesus.

I command all spirits operating in my blood and circulatory systems to come out in the name of Jesus.

I command all spirits operating in my muscles and muscular system to come out in the name of Jesus.

I command all religious spirits of doubt, unbelief, error, heresy, and tradition that came in through religion to come out in the name of Jesus.

I command all spirits from my past that are hindering my present and future to come out in the name of Jesus.

I command all ancestral spirits that entered through my ancestors to come out in the name of Jesus.

I command all hidden spirits hiding in any part of my life to come out in the name of Jesus.

PRAYERS FOR BINDING AND LOOSING

I have the keys of the kingdom, and whatever I bind on earth is bound in heaven, and whatever I loose on earth is loosed in heaven (Matt. 16:19).

I bind the kings in chains and the nobles with fetters of iron (Ps. 149:8).

I bind the strongman and spoil his goods (Matt. 12:29).

I bind leviathan and all proud spirits arrayed against my life (Job 41:5).

I bind the principalities, powers, rulers of the darkness of this world, and spiritual wickedness in high places (Eph. 6:12).

I bind all sickness and disease released against my mind or body.

Let the exiles be loosed (Isa. 51:14).

Let the prisoners be loosed (Ps. 146:7).

Loose those appointed to death (Ps. 102:20).

I loose my neck from all bands (Isa. 52:2).

I loose myself from the bands of wickedness (Isa. 58:6).

I loose myself from the bands of Orion (Job 38:31).

I loose myself from all bonds (Ps. 116:16).

I loose my mind, will, and emotions from every assignment and spirit of darkness in the name of Jesus.

I loose my city and region from every assignment of hell.

I loose my finances from every spirit of poverty, debt, and lack.

I loose myself from all generational curses and hereditary spirits (Gal. 3:13).

I loose myself from every assignment of witchcraft, sorcery, and divination.

I loose myself from every spoken curse and negative word spoken against my life.

I loose my hands from iniquity.

I loose my feet from mischief.

I loose my neck and shoulder from all yokes and heavy burdens.

I loose my eyes from seeing evil.

I loose my tongue from speaking perverseness.

I loose my ears from hearing evil.

I loose my mind from thinking evil.

I loose my will from stubbornness and rebellion.

I loose my emotions from hurts and wounds.

I loose my sexual character from lust and perversion.

I loose my physical body from sickness and disease.

I loose my memory from traumatic experiences of the past.

I loose my appetite from addiction.

I loose my heart from all hardness, unbelief, doubt, and fear.

I loose my wrist and ankles from all chains and shackles.

I loose my conscience from all guilt and condemnation, legalism, and religious bondage.

CHAPTER 5

DESTROYING STUBBORN DEMONS AND STRONGHOLDS

If you have faith as a mustard seed, you will say to this mountain, "Move from here to there," and it will move; and nothing will be impossible for you. However, this kind does not go out except by prayer and fasting.

—MATTHEW 17:20–21

G OD WANTS TO break and destroy some stubborn stuff in your life. Deliverance from all your enemies is a benefit of walking in covenant with God. He wants to set you free from all the wiles of the devil, even the ones you think you will never be free of. I'm talking about stubborn problems that don't seem to move or break no matter how much you pray and war, stuff that just doesn't seem to let go. A lot of people have become frustrated and discouraged because it just wears them out. But God has a plan for your deliverance, a way of escape out of the snares and traps of the enemy. The Lord says:

> *"In an acceptable time I have heard you, and in the day of salvation I have helped you."* Behold, now is the accepted time; behold, *now is the day of salvation*.
>
> —2 CORINTHIANS 6:2, EMPHASIS ADDED

> Do not be afraid. Stand firm and you will see the deliverance the LORD will bring you today.
>
> —EXODUS 14:13, NIV

"THIS KIND"

There are different kind of demons. Some demons are very easy to cast out of your life. Some demons always put up a fight. It takes a lot more strength and anointing to break their power. In Matthew 17 there is the story of the man who brought his child to the disciples of Jesus and they could not cure him.

> And Jesus rebuked the demon, and it came out of him; and the child was cured from that very hour. Then the disciples came to Jesus privately and said, "Why could we not cast him out?" So Jesus said to them, "Because of your unbelief; for assuredly, I say to you, if you have faith as a mustard seed, you will say to this mountain, 'Move from here to there,' and it will move; and nothing will be impossible for you. However, this kind does not go out except by prayer and fasting."
> —Matthew 17:18–21

The scripture says "this kind." This means there are different kinds of demons. Some demons are stronger than others. Some demons are more stubborn and defiant than others. There are a lot of reasons why a spirit can be stubborn in a person's life.

Sometimes these things can be so deeply rooted, strong, and stubborn, because not only have they been in your life but they have also been in your family's life for generations. Sometimes a demon in a person's life is like a plant that has a complex root system. The deeper the roots go in the soil, the harder it is to pull up the plant. And sometimes people have had spirits in their lives for so many years until they have developed a strong root systems. When they try to pull them out, they don't come out by just tugging at it. They need to get in the root system and cut it and then pull them out.

If you have a green thumb or have done any gardening, then you know all weeds are not the same. You can come across a weed and pull and pull and that thing won't budge. It's been there so long and its roots go deep into the soil.

When I say "stubborn," I am not referring to stubbornness, which is a demon in itself. I am referring to a spirit that is very difficult to remove. Jesus gives us the key, which is prayer and fasting. If you are having any of these issues in your life, I believe that prayer and fasting are the way to break their power and drive them out of your life. There is just no way around it.

Here are some spirits that I've come across that can be classified as stubborn.

Religious spirit

One of the most stubborn demons I have seen is a religious spirit—a spirit that causes people to reject change and growth. It causes them to stubbornly hold on to teachings that are not of God. It's hard to teach people who have been taught a certain way all their lives. The religious spirit causes people to be some of the most stubborn people you'll ever meet. One of the things a religious spirit needs to be faced with is that as we grow in God, our revelation of God grows. All of us have to change. We cannot stubbornly hold on to teaching that is contrary to Scripture. We must be humble enough to admit that we don't know everything. All of us are growing and learning. All of us have to change.

There are a lot of things I could talk about that I have had to change in my life in the last years of ministry. And there are things I had to come to grips with that I even preached, that sounded good but weren't really accurate—and I had to change them, because God gave me further light and understanding. Religious spirits can be so stubborn.

Lust

Lust is a strong-rooted spirit because it is rooted in the flesh. The longer a person has been in a lifestyle—homosexuality, adultery, masturbation—the more difficult it is. That thing will stubbornly cling to your flesh. Sometimes fasting is the way to weaken the root system because when you fast, you are dealing with the flesh. You are subduing your flesh. That's why demons hate fasting. They don't want you to fast. But if you truly want to be free, I recommend that you fast.

Addictions

This spirit is also rooted deeply in the flesh. I've dealt with people who just could not quit smoking. It's difficult for them to get delivered from just a smoking habit. They do everything to break it. They pray. They come for deliverance. They just can't break it. It's a stubborn spirit. Sometimes they get frustrated, and the enemy condemns them and tells them, "You're not strong." But sometimes you have to fast when you are trying to break free from a spirit of addiction, because it is so rooted in the flesh.

All addictions operate in similar ways—drugs, alcohol, gluttony, eating disorders, food addictions. They must be broken through fasting and prayer.

Bitterness

Bitterness is often the result of rejection and hurt. People become angry and bitter when they fail to forgive and release people who have wounded and offended them. Everyone has experienced some sort of pain in life, and many do not resolve it and, therefore, end up becoming bitter. Bitterness is a deep-rooted spirit. It goes deep into a person's emotions and is hard to dislodge because the person "feels" angry and other deep emotions that are so real to them. This demon gets rooted down into the flesh. Reacting in anger or revisiting the bitterness satisfies the flesh. This is why the root of bitterness needs to be broken through fasting, which starves the flesh. Bitterness is very common, and multitudes need deliverance from it.

Anger

Anger can be a stubborn demon. Some people just can't seem to overcome anger. They erupt, but feel so guilty.

Poverty—lack, debt, financial struggles

There are believers who give. They believe God. They feel so bad because they can't seem to get a financial breakthrough. They can't seem to get employment or opportunities for their business. They can't seem to overcome, and they get depressed. They begin to feel as though they don't have enough faith, maybe they don't believe God enough, or maybe they're not saved like someone else, maybe they aren't close to God, maybe God doesn't like them, maybe God doesn't favor them the way He favors others. Well, it could be a stubborn spirit of poverty that's been in their family for generations—a curse or a generational spirit and that thing just will not let go. But I believe that with God nothing is impossible. It may be time to fast and pray until breakthrough comes. When you are dealing with a stubborn demon, you cannot give up.

FACING GOLIATH

When we face stubborn demons and strongholds, it's as if we are facing Goliaths. All of Israel was intimidated by Goliath because he was a giant. He challenged anybody to come down and fight him for forty days and forty nights. Nobody met the challenge until David showed up. David said, "Who is this uncircumcised Philistine who would dare to defy the armies of the living God? I'll go and fight him!" (See 1 Samuel 17:26.) David was a fighter. And I pray the spirit of David would come upon you in this hour. Every time a Goliath stands up and challenges you, I pray that you will say, "God has not given me the spirit of fear but of power and love and a sound mind." And as David did, may you not only kill the enemy but also cut off his head!

Think about David's weapons. He tried to use King Saul's armor, but it was too big and heavy. He went to battle with his own little slingshot. A slingshot? Against a giant? Sometimes the weapons God gives us to fight with and defeat the enemy are most unusual. But "the weapons of our warfare are not carnal but mighty in God for pulling down strongholds" (2 Cor. 10:4). Use the weapon of praise. Use the weapon of worship. Use the weapon of the Word. Use the weapon of prayer and fasting. Declare: "I am not trying to do this in my flesh. God, I pray. I fast. I humble myself before You. I know that it's not by might nor by power but by the Spirit of the Lord that every mountain be removed from my life!"

It is time to be free from every stubborn devil and stubborn person who tries to keep you from doing what God has called you to do. Stand up and say, "No, devil, 'this kind' *will* leave. I will pray and fast until I get a breakthrough. Because I will not allow anything to stop me from doing what God has assigned for me to do."

DON'T LOSE HOPE

One of my favorite Scriptures is, "Hope deferred makes the heart sick, but when the desire comes, it is a tree of life" (Prov. 13:12). In other words, when you have hope for something to come to pass but it keeps getting deferred, you get discouraged and feel like giving up. But when the desire comes and you get what you had been hoping and believing for, you feel alive and invigorated—fulfilled. The Bible calls this "a tree of life."

One of the keys to enjoying life, the abundant life, and enjoying the life in God is to have your hopes come to pass. When you are always left in a place of hoping and hoping, this deferral turns into hopelessness, discouragement, frustration, depression, and torment. When people can't seem to get breakthrough in particular areas, they just give up. Some have left church or left God because this thing they were hoping would break through was so stubborn and would not move in their lives. But I am committed to seeing stubborn demons and strongholds destroyed. No matter how strong or stubborn a demon is, God still has all power!

One of the most defiant and stubborn animals is the mule. If mules don't want to do something, you can't make them do it. They just dig in. You have to drag them. My prayer is that through this book and others to follow, I am giving you tools and strategies from God to deal with mule spirits, donkey demons, and all those demons that say no when you say come out (sometimes they say no before you say come out). They will come out in the name of Jesus and through prayer and fasting.

Long War

> Now there was a long war between the house of Saul and the house of David. But David grew stronger and stronger, and the house of Saul grew weaker and weaker.
> —2 Samuel 3:1

You may not like this term *long war*. I don't blame you. Who would? We want it to end quickly. But some wars don't end quickly. If you are fighting a stubborn enemy who refuses to give in to surrender, then just know it is going to fight and fight and fight. There are demons who fight and fight and fight to hold on. But I have good news for you. If you keep putting pressure on the enemy, you will get stronger and stronger, and he will get weaker and weaker.

What demons cannot handle is a long war. They want you to hit them and give up. But you have the mentality that you will continue in prayer, fasting, and putting pressure on this demon, because it is just a matter of time before it breaks!

Sometimes you have to weaken demons. We have experienced this in our deliverance ministry at Crusaders Church. We've dealt with demons that are very strong. Over a period of time we will pray, fast, rebuke, and hold several sessions dealing with the same demon, but after a while we'll see that demon getting weaker and weaker.

When you first start praying for deliverance from some demonic spirits, they will tell you, "We aren't going. You can't cancel/cast us out. You don't have power. We're going to stay here. We are going to destroy. You belong to us. This is our house." You just say, "OK. Just keep talking. I'm going to pray—pray in tongues, fast, rebuke the devil, plead the blood, quote scriptures…" Then after a while those same tough-talking demons will say, "Would you leave us alone? Would you give it a break? You are getting on our nerves." You can always tell when demons are starting to weaken, because they get angry and start threatening. They'll say, "We're going to kill you." Don't be afraid. That's called panic. When you start seeing the devil panic, you know that you need to keep putting on the pressure until he whimpers out of your life.

Just because it's a long war does not mean you are losing. People have asked me why God would allow these things to stay in our lives for a long war. God allows it because He wants to teach us how to fight. You learn faith and persistence in long war. You need that as a child of God. You need to learn how to stand in faith against impossible situations. You don't look at how it looks. You need to believe God.

When God sent Israel into the land to drive out the enemy, they did not drive all of them out in one year. God didn't let them drive all of the enemies out of the land in one year. A verse in Judges 3 says that God left some of the nations in Canaan to teach Israel how to fight, how to war. Many of the ones that came out of Egypt knew nothing about warfare.

Sometimes as you are battling darkness, the Lord is teaching you how to war, how to use your faith, how to use the Word, how to use prayer, how to stand. He wants to teach you how to fight so you will not be a wimp in the army of the Lord. The greatest warriors in God's kingdom are people who have had to fight battles for themselves and overcome some things. When you overcome stuff, it is no longer a theory from the Bible. You know that victory is real. You know how to achieve victory. That gives you much better ability to fight for other people, to war for other people, to use your faith, to develop your strength in the Lord. Sometimes your personal victories set you up to be able to help someone else get victory.

A lot of believers don't like a long war. They give up. This is what the enemy is counting on. He is hoping the people of God will get tired and quit. What he wants us to feel is that we can't do it, that we can't defeat him, and that we won't win. He wants to bluff us that we are not strong enough. But I say to you, don't give up. Don't roll over and die. If God be for you, who can be against you (Rom. 8:31)? God is on your side. You may have to fight for what's yours, and it may take some time. But when you pray and fast and commit to seeing victory no matter how long it takes, it is only a matter of time until the enemy will break, and you *will* have victory.

No, Three Times Is Not the Charm

In 2 Kings 13:14–19 we are introduced to the arrow of deliverance and learn how the prophetic anointing helps us to war.

> Elisha had become sick with the illness of which he would die. Then Joash the king of Israel came down to him, and wept over his face, and said, "O my father, my father, the chariots of Israel and their horsemen!" And Elisha said to him, "Take a bow and some arrows." So he took himself a bow and some arrows. Then he said to the king of Israel, "Put your hand on the bow." So he put his hand on it, and Elisha put his hands on the king's hands. And he said, "Open the east window"; and he opened it. Then Elisha said, "Shoot"; and he shot. And he said, "The arrow of the Lord's deliverance and the arrow of deliverance from Syria; for *you must strike the Syrians at Aphek till you have destroyed them.*" Then he said, "Take the arrows"; so he took them. And he said to the king of Israel, "Strike the ground"; so he struck three times,

and stopped. And the man of God was angry with him, and said, "You should have struck five or six times; then you would have struck Syria till you had destroyed it! But now you will strike Syria only three times."

—EMPHASIS ADDED

I believe we can war according to prophecy. The word of the Lord is what you need to win and achieve victory. It is important to be connected to the prophetic. The words encourage us in what we are dealing with. It helps us to war against our enemies and win. The Syrians were the major enemies of Israel. They were a very strong and stubborn enemy. King Joash come to a sick and dying prophet Elisha and cries out to him about the armies of Syria. Elisha tells Joash that he must strike against Syria over and over again until they have been destroyed. Then Elisha tells him to take a bow and arrows and strike it on the ground. He didn't tell him how many times. Joash hit it on the ground three times and stopped. The prophet was angry, because now that would be how many times he would defeat the Syrians.

Three times was not enough to destroy the Syrians as Elisha had prophesied. Perhaps Elisha could have told him how many times to strike the arrows on the ground. But sometimes what is in a person comes out in their actions. Joash didn't have enough hatred and anger for the enemy to strike and strike the ground beyond the third time and maybe until the arrow broke!

When you are dealing with the enemy, you need to give him more than just a courtesy tap. You need to really want to win. You have to hate what you are fighting so much that you beat it until the arrows break. You have to hate lust, poverty, fear, rejection, or whatever it is until you smash it. It's not just one, two, three, and then look at the prophet and ask, "Did I do good?" No! Strike it until it is destroyed!

Another principle: sometimes it takes more than one victory before you completely consume the enemy. It wasn't just one battle; it was more than one. In essence the prophet said, "You should have stuck four or five times to completely consume the enemy. Now you will only win three times." And evidently three victories would not be enough to completely destroy the Syrians. The Syrians lost, but they were still in a position to rebuild. We want to destroy the enemy so that he can't rebuild anymore. We want to mess up his strongholds so much that they are destroyed, and we don't have to worry about seeing that thing again.

STUBBORN PHARAOHS

> Do not be afraid. Stand firm and you will see the deliverance the LORD will bring you today. The Egyptians you see today you will *never see again*.
> —EXODUS 14:13, NIV, EMPHASIS ADDED

Pharaoh is the type of the devil. He was stubborn. He kept hardening his heart. He kept changing his mind. No matter how much judgment came, he kept hardening his heart. But finally God had one thing to break him—he took his firstborn. But Pharaoh still came after them, but God said, "Don't worry about him; I am going to drown him in the sea, and you will see him no more!"

I pray that every pharaoh, every stubborn pharaoh, be drowned and you will not see him again! You may have to go on a fast not one time; you may have to fast ten times. It took ten plagues to break Pharaoh's power. It's time to break those stubborn pharaohs. Sometimes a pharaoh may be a person—controlling devil, witch, warlock, Jezebel, a person who wants to control your life, your church.

I hate to use this example, but it is what comes to my mind. In the *Wizard of Oz*, when the Wicked Witch of the East threatened the other one, she laughed and said, "Ha, ha, ha! Rubbish. You have no power here!" In the same way you need to laugh at the devil. When the devil threatens you, just laugh, "Ha, ha, ha! Rubbish. You have no power here!" I watch that movie just to see that. I know that's one witch talking to another, but just eliminate the witch part, and you'll get it.

Don't let those demon spirits threaten you! I don't care if they are flying around the room on a broom with a black hat on. Declare: "No witch, no warlock, and no Jezebel will control my life. I am a servant of Jesus Christ, and whom the Son sets free is free indeed. No apostle, no doctor apostle, no bishop, no archbishop, no archbishop deluxe…I don't care what your title is… no prophet, no prophetess, whatever, you not called to control my life. You are not called to dominate me and manipulate me and intimidate me. The devil is a liar!"

Sometimes it takes more than one judgment, battle, or victory to break stubborn enemies. There is something about stubborn enemies. You can hit them one time, but they keep coming back. It seemed that no matter what God did to loosen Pharaoh's grip on the children of Israel, he would not let God's people go. Even Pharaoh's advisors told him, "This is the finger of God. You cannot fight God." (See Exodus 8:19.) And eventually even he had to bow his knee to the King of kings.

It is time to put a hurting on the devil. We are not going to leave them alone, even as they cry out, "Let us alone" (Mark 1:23–24, KJV). We are going to put pressure on them. We are going to bind, rebuke, cast out, pray, and deal with the powers of hell. They have been left alone for too long. Nobody was praying, fasting, taking authority, or preaching. They have had full sway in the generations. They did what they wanted to do. But now there is a new breed being raised up. There are pastors, prophets, apostles, teachers, evangelists, and everyday believers who will not leave the enemy alone until he is gone!

Prayers to Break Stubborn
Demons and Strongholds

I bind, rebuke, and cast out every stubborn demon that would attempt to stubbornly hold on to my life in the name of Jesus.

I come against every stubborn stronghold and command it to yield to the power of God and the name of Jesus (2 Sam. 5:7).

I put pressure on every stubborn demon and stronghold and break its grip in my life in the name of Jesus.

I uproot every stubborn root from my life in the name of Jesus (Matt. 15:13).

I command every stubborn, ironlike yoke to shatter and break in the name of Jesus (Judg. 1:19).

I break the power of every proud, stubborn, and arrogant demon that exalts itself against Christ, and command it to be abased, in the name of Jesus.

I break the power of all iniquity in my family that would stubbornly attempt to control my life in the name of Jesus.

I come against all obstinate demons and break their influence in my life in the name of Jesus.

I rebuke all stubborn, habitual patterns of failure and frustration in my life in the name of Jesus.

I rebuke all stubborn pharaohs that would attempt to hold God's people, and I command you to let God's people go, in the name of Jesus (Exod. 8:32).

I bind and rebuke all stubborn enemies, who stubbornly oppose me and my progress, in the name of Jesus.

I rebuke all stubborn demons that would attempt to resist the power of God and the authority I have through Jesus Christ, and I render you powerless to resist, in the name of Jesus.

I come against every persistent pattern that limits me, and I render it powerless against me, in the name of Jesus.

There is nothing impossible through faith, and I release my faith against every stubborn and obstinate demon, and I resist you steadfastly, in the name of Jesus (Matt. 19:26).

I weaken, break down, and pressure every stubborn demon and stronghold. You are getting weaker and weaker, and I am getting stronger and stronger. I exercise long war against you, until you are completely defeated and destroyed from my life in the name of Jesus (2 Sam. 3:1).

I lay siege against every stubborn stronghold through prayer and fasting, until your walls come down in the name of Jesus (Deut. 20:19).

I use the battering ram of prayer and fasting to demolish all the gates of every stubborn stronghold in the name of Jesus. Let every Jericho wall fall through my praise, as I lift my voice as a trumpet against you in the name of Jesus (Josh. 6:1, 20).

Let every demonic stump be removed from my life in the name of Jesus.

I break the will of every stubborn spirit that would attempt to remain in my life in the name of Jesus. You have no will to remain, your will is broken, and you must submit to the name of Jesus and the power of the Holy Ghost.

I come against all stubborn demons and strongholds in my family that have refused to leave, and I assault every demonic fortress that has been built for generations, in the name of Jesus.

I rebuke every stubborn mule and bull of Bashan from my life in the name of Jesus. I break your will against me in the name of Jesus. You are defeated and must bow to the name above all names (Ps. 22:12).

The anointing is increasing in my life through prayer and fasting, and every stubborn yoke is being destroyed (Isa. 10:27).

NEVER AGAIN CONFESSIONS

Never again will Pharaoh (Satan) control me, because I have been delivered from his power.

Never again will I allow the devil to do what he desires in my life, but I resist the devil, and he flees from me (James 4:7).

Never again will I listen to or believe the lies of the devil, for he is a liar and the father of lies (John 8:44).

Never again will I be vexed by unclean spirits (Luke 6:18, KJV).

Never again will I be harassed by the enemy (Matt. 9:36, AMP).

Never again will I be bound, for Christ has made me free. I am free indeed (John 8:36).

Never again will I allow the demons of double-mindedness to confuse me and make me indecisive (James 1:8).

Never again will I allow curses to hinder my life. I break every curse, for I have been redeemed from the curse (Gal. 3:13).

Never again will I open the door for demons to come into my life through unforgiveness (Matt. 18:35).

Never again will I open the door for demons to enter my life through habitual sin.

Never again will I open the door for demons to enter my life through occult involvement.

Never again will I open the door for demons to enter through rebellion and disobedience.

Never again will the demon of mind control affect my thinking. I sever all the tentacles of mind control.

Never again will serpent and scorpion spirits affect my life, for I have power to tread on serpents and scorpions.

Never again will the enemy be my master; Jesus is my Lord.

Never again will I tolerate the works of the devil in my life, for Jesus came and destroyed the works of the devil (1 John 3:8).

Never again will I compromise my standards and holiness; the Word of God is my standard, not the standards of the world (2 Cor. 10:2, NIV).

Never again will I allow the enemy to control any part of my life, but my life is under the control of the Spirit and Word of God.

Never again will I allow the enemy to control my destiny, but God is the revealer and finisher of my destiny.

Never again will I allow the enemy to abort any plan of God for my life.

Never again will I allow people to draw me away from the love of God, but I commit myself to walking in love, for God is love (1 John 4:7–8).

Never again will I shut up my bowels of compassion (1 John 3:17, KJV).

Never again will I behave unseemly, for love does not behave unseemly (1 Cor. 13:5, KJV).

Never again will I be easily provoked, for love is not easily provoked (1 Cor. 13:5).

Never again will I seek my own, for love does not seek its own (1 Cor. 13:5).

Never again will I think evil, for love does not think evil (1 Cor. 13:5).

Never again will I lose hope, for love hopes all things (1 Cor. 13:7).

Never again will I give up, for love endures all things (1 Cor. 13:7).

Never again will I allow the accuser to accuse me, for I am washed and cleansed by the blood of the Lamb (Rev. 1:5; 7:14).

Never again will I allow sorrow and sadness to control my soul, for the Lord has taken away my sorrow and pain (Isa. 65:19).

Never again will the heavens be shut over my life, but the Lord has opened the windows of heaven (Mal. 3:10).

CHAPTER 6
HOW TO FAST FOR DELIVERANCE

"Now, therefore," says the LORD, "Turn to Me with all your heart, with fasting, with weeping, and with mourning." So rend your heart, and not your garments; return to the LORD your God, for He is gracious and merciful, slow to anger, and of great kindness; and He relents from doing harm.

—JOEL 2:12–13

YOU'VE COMMANDED, REBUKED, prayed prayers, done warfare, and shouted, but there's more that needs to be broken off your life. It's time to add some fasting to your warfare strategy. There are just those "kinds" of demonic strongholds that there is no other way around them. No shortcuts. You have to fast and humble yourself until that thing breaks and leaves your life.

As I mentioned in the previous chapter, demons are different in terms of their wickedness. There are demons that are more wicked, more unclean, stronger, more stubborn, and higher in rank, ability, and intelligence. The longer a demon has been in a family or in a person's life, the harder it is to remove because its roots go very deep. Demons such as rebellion, pride, witchcraft, Jezebel, poverty, and lack may only come out with a high level of faith.

Sometimes it seems as if they cannot be dislodged, and people will get discouraged and frustrated and feel they have failed. In Matthew 17 the disciples of Jesus encountered a demon in a young boy and could not cure him because of unbelief. Unbelief hinders us from dealing with strongholds. It takes faith to dislodge the enemy. Fasting helps you overcome unbelief and build strong faith.

83

This is the supernatural combination that Jesus gave His disciples in Matthew 17: prayer and fasting. I am not saying that when you fast you will earn brownie points with God or that you are working your way to enjoying God's blessings. We don't fast to be saved, please God, or to go to heaven. There is no law that says if you don't fast you will go to hell. We fast for breakthrough and revival, for family and loved ones. For the weapons of our warfare are not carnal but mighty through God!

Some things take fasting *and* prayer. There is no other way around. There are those kinds of demons that just don't give up. They are strong, proud, arrogant, and defiant. They are familiar spirits that have been in your family. But you have to get to the point that you don't care how messed up your family is; you say, "It is stopping with me. This is not going on to another generation. This is it, devil. If my grandmother or grandfather didn't stand against it, if my mother and father didn't defeat it, I'm going to defeat it. I refuse to be poor, broke, sick, rejected, messed up....No!"

Sometimes you have to do something unusual, extraordinary, and beyond the norm to see breakthrough. Normal church, normal Christianity, normal preaching, and normal praying are not going to get the job done. Some little sweet prayer is not going to do. Religion won't get it done. It is going to take an anointing that destroys the yoke. When you fast, the anointing increases in your life because you are so into the Spirit. The authority of God, power of God, and faith of God comes alive when you lay aside some things and fast. You will find yourself getting stronger and stronger. Shouting doesn't do it. It is the anointing that does it.

Isaiah 58 talks about how we can fast to break every yoke to undo the heavy burdens. Fasting makes room so that the oppressed go free. Fasting breaks bondages and causes revival. When you are dealing with a serious issue—maybe you are dealing with something you don't know how to handle—the best thing to do sometimes is to let go of some food for a little while. Pray against that thing. Man may not be able to help you, and you may not know how to defeat it, but with God all things are possible.

As you fast and humble yourself, the grace of God will come upon your life. The Lord will be the strength of your life. What you could not do in the flesh, you can do by the Spirit of God. Because it's not by might nor by power, but by the Spirit of the Lord that every mountain is removed!

Listen, extraordinary situations require extraordinary measures. Sometimes it only happens when you get desperate—when you are so tired of being defeated and hindered in an area.

Let's see some victories we haven't seen before. Let's get some breakthroughs we haven't had before. Let's see some miracles we haven't seen before. Let's drive out some demons we haven't driven out before. Let's see some curses broken that would not leave. Let's see some generational stuff uprooted that could not be uprooted. Let's see a change! Not once. Not twice. Not even three times. If you have to go more than that, go more than that. Don't give up. Keep doing it. Keep going until you know you have victory, until you have breakthrough, until you sense something breaking!

You have to get so tired of the devil that you say, "Enough is enough. If I have to turn my plate down to get a breakthrough in this area, I won't eat." When your stomach starts screaming out, tell it to back up. In the end you will win, and you will have victory! Let our spiritual enemies be smitten and consumed in Jesus's name!

You have to be determined: "No demon is going to control my life. I am a child of God, and who the Son sets free is free indeed. I don't care how stubborn this thing is, how it tries to hang on. I am going to break every finger and the thumbs of the enemy. I'm going to break his wrists, break his grip. . . . Devil, you cannot have my life!"

This is the faith and unshakable resolve fasting will build in your life to see deliverance in every area the enemy has tried to control. Let's look at even more benefits fasting will add to your life.

Fasting Releases the Breaker Anointing

We have established that there are some things in our lives that just can't stay around if we are to walk victoriously and in covenant with God. We have gone too long and too soft with the enemy wreaking havoc in our lives. Fasting can release the breaker anointing. The prophet Micah prophesied the day of the breaker coming up before his people. We are living in the days of the breaker.

> The breaker is come up before them: they have broken up, and have passed through the gate, and are gone out by it: and their king shall pass before them, and the Lord on the head of them.
>
> —Micah 2:13, kjv

The Lord is a breaker. He is able to break through any obstacle or opposition on behalf of His covenant people. There is a breaker anointing arising upon the church. We are seeing and experiencing more breakthroughs than ever before. Fasting will cause breakthroughs to continue in families, cities, nations, finances, church growth, salvation, healing, and deliverance. It will help believers to break through all opposition from the enemy.

As we have said, there are some spirits operating in our lives that cannot be overcome without fasting. Some believers struggle with certain limitations that they cannot seem to break through. A revelation for how covenant and fasting work hand in hand will change this and result in victories that would not ordinarily be obtained. A life of consistent fasting will cause many victories to manifest. God's will is that His covenant believers live a life of victory and perfect peace with nothing being impossible to them.

APPROACH FASTING WITH
HUMILITY AND SINCERITY

In Jesus's day the Pharisees fasted with attitudes of pride and superiority:

> The Pharisee stood and prayed thus with himself, God, I thank thee, that I am not as other men are....I fast twice in the week...
>
> —LUKE 18:11–12, KJV

Anytime you are full of pride, being legalistic and religious, you can fast and pray all you want, but you won't see many miracles. The Pharisees didn't have any miracles come as a result of their prayer and fasting. They had no power. Jesus had all the miracles because He was humble and full of mercy, love, and compassion toward people.

The Pharisees had nothing but long robes on, robes with no miracles. They couldn't heal a headache. They couldn't heal a mosquito bite. They couldn't heal a hangnail. They had no power because they were not humble and showed no mercy. Jesus showed up and broke all their rules. He healed the sick, raised the dead, and cast out devils. Then they wanted to kill him. They were not concerned about people. They were more concerned about their position and their title. Don't ever get to a place where your position or title takes the humility and the mercy of God out of your life. Always be humble. Always be merciful.

We must approach fasting with humility. Fasting must be genuine and not religious or hypocritical. This is what God requires in fasting. We must have correct motives in fasting. Fasting is a powerful tool if done correctly. Muslims and Hindus fast, but their fasts are merely religious. Great miracles and breakthroughs happen when fasting is done in the right spirit.

Isaiah chapter 58 describes the fast that God has chosen:

- Fasting cannot be done with amusement (v. 3).
- Fasting cannot be done while mistreating others (v. 3).
- Fasting cannot be done for strife or contention (v. 4).
- Fasting should cause one to bow his head in humility, like a bulrush (v. 5).
- Fasting should be a time of searching the heart and repenting.
- Fasting should be done with an attitude of compassion for the lost and hurting (v. 7).

This is the fast that God promises to bless.

The enemy knows the power of prayer and fasting, and he will do everything in his power to stop you. Believers who begin to fast can expect to encounter much spiritual resistance. A believer must be committed to a fasted lifestyle. The rewards of fasting far outweigh the obstacles of the enemy.

How to Fast

Fasting is beneficial whether you fast partially or fully. One-day fasts on a consistent basis will strengthen your spirit over time and give you the ability to disciple yourself for longer fasts. Three-day fasts with just water are a powerful way to see breakthroughs. Fasts longer than three days should be done by people with more experience in fasting.

I do not recommend long fasts unless there is an emergency or if one is led by the Holy Spirit to do so. Daniel fasted twenty-one days and saw a great breakthrough for his people (Dan. 9–10). Daniel was also a prophet, and God will use prophets to fast for different reasons to see breakthroughs. Jesus fasted forty days before beginning His ministry. I do know of people who have fasted forty days and have seen great breakthroughs.

A partial fast can include some food such as vegetables and can be done for long lengths. Complete fasts consist of only water, and water is important to cleanse the system of toxins that are released through fasting. The Holy Spirit will reveal to you when you need to fast. A fasted lifestyle is a powerful lifestyle.

BREAKTHROUGHS THAT COME FROM FASTING

As a covenant believer deliverance and freedom are part of your salvation package. The enemy fights you for this freedom. This is why we are in a battle. He continues to steal from you what has already been claimed for you. Jesus gave you the authority to stop him from taking your covenant blessings. When you can also begin to fast and pray for the enemy's hands to be taken off of your stuff, here is what you can expect to see broken off your life and the lives of your family members.

Fasting will break the spirit of poverty over your life and will prepare the way for prosperity (Joel 2:15, 18–19, 24–26).

The prophet Joel gave the people the proper response to the locust invasion. Locusts represent demons that devour. Locusts represent the spirits of poverty and lack. The locusts had come upon Israel and devoured the harvest. Joel encouraged the people to fast and repent. God promised to hear their prayers and answer by sending corn, wine, and oil.

Corn, wine, and oil represent prosperity, one of the signs of walking in covenant with God. Fasting breaks the spirit of poverty and releases the spirit of prosperity. I have seen countless numbers of believers struggle in the area of their finances. Prosperity is elusive to many. This is because the demons of poverty have not been bound through fasting and prayer.

In Deuteronomy 8:3, 7–9, 18 God allowed the people to hunger in the wilderness by feeding them with only manna. They ate manna for forty years. This preceded their entering the Promised

Land. Fasting helps prepare a believer for the good land. This is a land without scarceness. This is a land with no lack. Fasting humbles the soul (Ps. 35:13). God rewards those who fast (Matt. 6:18). Tremendous blessings are released for those who understand the power of fasting and do it.

Fasting is one of the ways we can break generational strongholds of poverty. Fasting prepares a believer for prosperity by bringing him or her into a place of humility. God has promised to exalt the humble (1 Pet. 5:6). Financial promotion is part of this exaltation. God gives grace (favor) to the humble (James 4:6). Favor is a part of financial prosperity. Fasting releases grace and favor upon a person's life. This will break the cycle of poverty and failure.

Fasting will break the power of fear that tries to oppress you (Joel 2:21).

Do you desire to see great things happen in your life and in your family? The Lord desires to do great things for His covenant people. Fasting will break the spirit of fear in your life and in your family's life and will prepare the way for great things to happen. These great things include signs and wonders.

Fasting will break the stronghold of sexual impurity.

Sexual sin is one of the hardest sins to break. Many believers struggle with generational lust that has passed down through the family lines. Lust spirits cause much shame, guilt, and condemnation. This robs the believer of the confidence and boldness he should have as a believer. Many believers struggle with masturbation, pornography, perversion, and fornication. Fasting for your family will drive these generational spirits from their lives.

In Judges 19:22 we read about some men in a city who wanted to have sexual relations with the guest of an old man in that city. They were homosexuals who were identified as sons of Belial. The man of the house tried to discourage them and offered them his daughter and the guest's concubine instead. The men took the concubine of the guest and abused her all night. The abuse was so severe that she died. The guest then took a knife and cut the concubine into twelve pieces and sent them to every tribe in Israel. His concubine had been raped to death.

The men who raped the concubine were from the tribe of Benjamin. The men of Israel gathered against the city and requested they turn over the guilty men. The children of Benjamin would not listen and instead gathered themselves to battle. The children of Benjamin destroyed twenty-two thousand men of Israel on the first day (Judg. 20:21), and they destroyed eighteen thousand on the second day (v. 25).

> Then all the children of Israel, and all the people, went up, and came unto the house of God, and wept, and sat there before the Lord, and fasted that day until even, and offered burnt offerings and peace offerings before the Lord...and [then] the Lord smote Benjamin before Israel.
>
> —Judges 20:26, 35, kjv

Israel could not overcome Benjamin until they fasted. The resistance of Benjamin implies that there was something demonic behind them. Twelve tribes could not overcome one tribe because of this demonic resistance. This resistance was broken after fasting. This was the only way perversion was rooted out of the tribe of Benjamin. Fasting helps you and your family break free from the chains of sexual perversion and lust.

Fasting will break the power of sickness and infirmity and release healing in your life (Isa. 58:5–6, 8).

Many believers struggle with sicknesses such as cancer, diabetes, high blood pressure, sinus problems, and chronic pain. These spirits of infirmity are often generational. Fasting helps eliminate chronic sickness and diseases. God has promised that our health will spring forth speedily.

Fasting will release God's glory for your protection (Isa. 58:8)

Divine protection is another promise from Isaiah 58. God promises to protect us with His glory. Fasting releases the glory of the Lord, which covers us. God has promised to cover the church with glory as a defense (Isa. 4:5). The enemy cannot penetrate or overcome this glory.

Fasting will result in answered prayer (Isa. 58:9).

Demonic interference causes many prayers to be hindered. Daniel fasted twenty-one days to break through demonic resistance and receive answers to his prayers. (See Daniel 10.) The prince of Persia withstood the answers for twenty-one days. Daniel's fast helped an angel to break through and bring the answers.

Fasting will cause many answers to prayer to be accelerated. These include prayers for salvation of loved ones and deliverance. Fasting helps to break the frustration of unanswered prayer.

Fasting releases divine guidance (Isa. 58:11).

Many believers have difficulty making correct decisions concerning relationships, finances, and ministry. This causes setbacks and wasted time because of foolish decisions. Fasting will help believers make correct decisions by releasing divine guidance. Fasting eliminates confusion. Fasting causes clarity and releases understanding and wisdom to make correct decisions.

Fasting is recommended for those who are making important decisions such as marriage and ministry choices.

Fasting will break generational curses (Isa. 58:12).

Many of the obstacles believers encounter are generational. Generational curses result from the iniquity of the fathers. Generational sins such as pride, rebellion, idolatry, witchcraft, occult involvement, Masonry, and lust open the door for evil spirits to operate in families through generations. Demons of destruction, failure, poverty, infirmity, lust, and addiction are major strongholds in the lives of millions of people.

Fasting helps loose the bands of wickedness. Fasting lets the oppressed go free. Fasting helps us to rebuild the old waste places. Fasting reverses the desolation that results from sin and rebellion.

Fasting closes breaches and brings forth restoration and rebuilding (Isa. 58:12; Neh. 1:4).

There are many believers who need restoration. They need restoration in their families, finances, relationships, health, and walk with the Lord. Fasting is a part of restoration.

Fasting closes the breaches. Breaches are gaps in the wall that give the enemy an entry point into our lives. Breaches need to be repaired and closed. When the breaches are closed, the enemy no longer has as opening to attack.

Fasting also helps keep us on the right path (Isa. 58:12). Fasting helps to prevent us from going astray. Fasting will help those who have strayed from the right path to return. Fasting is a cure for backsliding.

Fasting helps us to walk in the good path (Prov. 2:9), the path of life (v. 19), the path of peace (Prov. 3:17), the old path (Jer. 6:16), and the straight path (Heb. 12:13). Fasting restores these paths and helps us to walk in them.

In Nehemiah 1 we see that Nehemiah's journey to restore and rebuild the walls in Jerusalem began with fasting. Fasting initiated the events that made his plans possible. Fasting will be an asset to anyone with a desire to see restoration in the lives of people who have experienced desolation.

Fasting helps restore and rebuild the walls in our lives that have been broken down. Walls are symbolic of protection and safety. A city without walls is open for attack from the enemy (Prov. 25:28). Fasting helps restore the walls of salvation (Isa. 60:18). Fasting helps restore watchmen to the walls (Isa. 62:6).

Fasting will cause you to have great victory against overwhelming odds (2 Chron. 20:3).

Jehoshaphat was facing the combined armies of Moab, Ammon, and Edom. He was facing overwhelming odds. Fasting helped him to defeat these enemies. Fasting helps us to have victory in the midst of defeat.

Jehoshaphat called a fast because he was afraid. Fear is another stronghold that many believers have difficulty overcoming. Fasting will break the power of the demon of fear. Spirits of terror, panic, fright, apprehension, and timidity can be overcome through fasting. Freedom from fear is a requirement to live a victorious lifestyle.

Fasting will prepare the way for you and your children and deliver you from enemies that lie in wait (Ezra 8:21, 31).

The prophet Ezra fasted because he recognized the danger of his mission. Fasting will protect you and your children from the plans of the enemy. Fasting will stop the ambush of the enemy. Fasting will cause your substance to be protected from the attack of the enemy.

Fasting will break the powers of carnality, division, and strife (Phil. 3:19).

Carnality is a problem in many families in the body of Christ. To be carnal means to be fleshly. It means to mind earthly things. We should not be controlled by the belly. Fasting takes the power away from the belly and strengthens the spirit.

To be carnally minded is death. To be spiritually minded is life and peace (Rom. 8:6). Carnality causes division and strife (1 Cor. 3:13). Carnality hinders believers from growing and coming into maturity. Carnality prevents believers from understanding the deeper truths of the Scriptures.

Fasting helps believers focus on spiritual things. Fasting breaks us free from the power of the flesh. Fasting increases spiritual discernment (1 Cor. 2:15).

Fasting will break the powers of pride, rebellion, and witchcraft (Ps. 35:13; Job 33:17–20).

Sickness can be a result of pride. Pain can also be a result of pride. Sickness often results in the loss of appetite. This is a forced fast. Fasting humbles the soul. Fasting helps us overcome the strongman of pride. Pride and rebellion are generational spirits that are often difficult to overcome.

Gluttony and drunkenness are signs of rebellion (Deut. 21:20). Rebellion is as the sin of witchcraft (1 Sam. 15:23). God humbled Israel in the wilderness by feeding them with only manna (Deut. 8:3). Israel lusted for meat in the wilderness. This was a manifestation of rebellion (Ps. 106:14–15).

Fasting will cause the joy and the presence of the Lord to return (Mark 2:20).

The presence of the bridegroom causes joy. Weddings are filled with joy and celebration. When a believer loses joy and the presence of the Lord, he or she needs to fast. Fasting causes the joy and presence of the Lord to return. No believer can live a victorious life without the presence of the bridegroom. The joy of the Lord is our strength (Neh. 8:10).

Fasting will release the power of the Holy Spirit for the miraculous to occur (Luke 4:14, 18).

Fasting increases the anointing and the power of the Holy Spirit in the life of a believer. Jesus ministered in power after fasting. He healed the sick and cast out devils. All believers are expected to do the same works (John 14:12). Fasting helps us to minister healing and deliverance to our families and others around us. Fasting helps us walk in the power of God. Fasting releases the anointing for miracles to happen in your and your family's lives.

Fasting breaks unbelief and doubt (Matt. 13:58; 17:20).

> And he did not many mighty works there because of their unbelief.
>
> —MATTHEW 13:58, KJV

> And Jesus said unto them, Because of your unbelief: for verily I say unto you, If ye have faith as a grain of mustard seed, ye shall say unto this mountain, Remove hence to yonder place; and it shall remove; and nothing shall be impossible unto you.
>
> —MATTHEW 17:20, KJV

Unbelief is an enemy to operating in the miraculous. Jesus could not operate in the power of God because of the unbelief of the people. The disciples could not cast out a strong demon because of unbelief.

It is important to drive unbelief from your life. And one of the ways this is accomplished is through prayer and fasting. Prayer and fasting help us clear obstacles to our faith and faith-filled actions.

In the healing revival of 1948–1957 many came into a healing ministry this way. Franklin Hall wrote a key book, *The Atomic Power With God With Prayer and Fasting*. He called fasting "supercharged prayer." He said the flesh had three primary needs or desires (food, sex, and status), and of these the need for food is dominant. These natural desires are valid, but they can easily become too strong (inordinate desires equal lusts) and dominate us. Thus fasting is the way to assert control on the flesh where it counts.

Fasting, coupled with prayer, is one of the most powerful weapons to breakthrough and overcome unbelief. Jesus preceded

His ministry with fasting and returned in the power of the Spirit into Galilee. Jesus did not struggle with unbelief, and He operated in faith throughout His ministry. When challenged with unbelief in any situation, I encourage you to fast and pray for breakthrough.

DECLARE THE BENEFITS OF FASTING OVER YOUR LIFE

Lord, I believe in the power of Your chosen fast (Isa. 58).

Lord, let my fasting destroy the yokes that the enemy has set up against me.

Let Your light come into my life through Your chosen fast.

Let health and healing be released to me though Your chosen fast.

Let me see breakthroughs of salvation and deliverance in my life through Your chosen fast.

Let miracles be released in my life through Your chosen fast.

Let Your power and authority be released in my life through Your chosen fast.

I humble my soul through fasting; let Your favor exalt me.

I drive every stubborn demon out of my life through Your chosen fast.

Let Your covenant blessing and mercy be released on me through Your chosen fast.

Nothing is impossible with You, Lord; let my impossibilities become possibilities through Your chosen fast.

Let every assignment of hell against me be broken through Your chosen fast.

Let all pride, rebellion, and witchcraft operating in my life be destroyed through Your chosen fast.

Let Your anointing increase in my life through Your chosen fast.

Let me enjoy restoration through Your chosen fast.

Let all carnality be rebuked from my life through Your chosen fast.

Let all habits and iniquity in me be broken and overcome through Your chosen fast.

Let my prayers be answered speedily through Your chosen fast.

Guide me through Your chosen fast.

Manifest Your glory to me through Your chosen fast.

Let the strongholds of sexual impurity and lust be broken in my life through Your chosen fast.

Let sickness and infirmity be destroyed in my life, and let healing come forth through Your chosen fast.

Let all poverty and lack be destroyed in my life through Your chosen fast.

Remove all oppression and torment from my life through Your chosen fast.

I humble myself with fasting (Ps. 35:13).

I will turn to the Lord with fasting, weeping, and mourning (Joel 2:12).

This "kind" that I face will go out from me through fasting and prayer (Matt. 17:21).

I will fast according the fast chosen by the Lord (Isa. 58:5).

I will proclaim a fast and humble myself before our God, to seek from Him the right way for my family and all our possessions (Ezra 8:21).

I fast to loose the bonds of wickedness, to undo heavy burdens, to the let the oppressed go free, and to break every yoke (Isa. 58:6).

I will set my face toward the Lord God to make requests by prayer and supplication, with fasting, sackcloth, and ashes (Dan. 9:3).

I will fast in the secret place, and my Father sees in secret. He will reward me openly (Matt. 6:18).

I will not depart from the temple of the Lord but will serve God with fastings and prayers night and day (Luke 2:37).

CHAPTER 7

MEDITATE ON THE WORD TO MAINTAIN YOUR DELIVERANCE

It is written, "Man shall not live by bread alone, but by
every word that proceeds from the mouth of God."

—MATTHEW 4:4

A S I STATED in chapter 2, it is not enough to just go through a deliverance session or two to maintain the proper spiritual diet that will support your walk with God. You also need the Word of God implanted in your heart so that you will not backslide and return to the things you have been set free from. Psalm 119:11 says, "Your word I have hidden in my heart, that I might not sin against You!"

I also mentioned in chapter 3 that one of the keys to being set free is light and revelation. You get revelation from studying and meditating on the Word of God. Revelation drives out the rulers of darkness that try to control your life. Revelation from the Word causes you to see what is hidden from the natural eye. Revelation will give you understanding of the mysteries of God. You will begin to walk in a level of understanding that is not common without revelation. This is a significant tool for victory in spiritual warfare and sustaining success in life.

Knowing things you couldn't know. Doing things you couldn't do. Going places you wouldn't know to go. Being in position for opportunities you couldn't have developed on your own. Supernatural wisdom and insight. Keen decision making and problem solving. Discerning the right time for things to happen. These are the mysterious things that God wants you to be ready to receive through His Word and through prophecy—His revealed word.

Maintaining your freedom from bondages and strongholds will allow your ear to be tuned to the voice of God and your mind to be aligned with the mind of Christ. Meditation on the Word keeps your spirit free from entanglements of the enemy and in tune, aligned, and walking the right path.

> Your word is a lamp to my feet and a light to my path.
> —PSALM 119:105

MEDITATION—KEY TO PROSPERITY AND SUCCESS

Being bound by demonic strongholds and oppressive spirits has a way of keeping you in a place of lack and failure. You may have a few high points here and there, but there is no lasting victory and success. When you are delivered by way of God's grace and mercy, you will find breakthrough from the cycles that keep you from lasting success and victory. When you are delivered and set free, you may even find that you will see success in many other areas that on the surface seem to be unrelated to what you were delivered from. Success, victory, and breakthrough become a way of life when you see true deliverance and learn to maintain that deliverance.

This is the covenant of God with you—that you will have the full measure of salvation so that you can walk free, have victory, take over the land that God swore to your fathers, and have good success in this life and the life to come. You cannot have good success when you are bound. By way of covenant you can be set free and walk in an abundance of prosperity and success.

Prosperity is not just about riches and fame. Prosperity covers everything that concerns you. When you are prosperous, you will not lack in health, relationships, supernatural power to serve and help others, wisdom, insight, knowledge, all the fruit of the Spirit, creativity, strategy for everyday life, as well as all of your needs being met. Do not get caught up into thinking that prosperity means that you will be a famous celebrity megachurch pastor or TV evangelist. Prosperity means that you will not lack *any* good thing the Lord has designed for you.

Joshua 1:8 gives insight on how we can make our way prosperous and have good success—which is essentially how to maintain our freedom and deliverance. The verse says that we must meditate in the Word *day and night*. This takes discipline, but it will pay off greatly if done consistently. Prosperity is the key benefit to being in covenant with God.

> In the Old Testament, there are several Hebrew words for the word 'meditate' but the main word is the word '*hagah*' which literally means 'mutter.'
>
> '*Hagah*' has been translated 'mutter' twice (Isa. 59:3; 8:19), 'meditate' six times (Jos. 1:8; Ps. 1:2; 63:6; 77:12; 143:5; Isa. 33:18). It has also been translated 'speak' four times (Ps. 35:28; 37:30; 115:7; Pro. 8:7), 'study' twice (Pro. 15:28; 24:2), 'talk' once (Ps. 71:24) and 'utter' once (Job 27:4).
>
> It can be noted from these Scriptures that meditation does indicate the use of the mouth as an instrument to mutter or speak God's Word. [1]

Muttering and meditating upon the Word of God, until it becomes alive in our spirits, is the key to actualizing the promises of God. Muttering (Hebrew *hagah,* "mutter") upon the Word of God day and night is likened to a tree planted by the rivers of water absorbing and drawing water into its system through its roots (Ps. 1:3).

> Joshua 1:8 says, "This book of the law shall not depart out of thy mouth." This does not mean you are to keep the Word in your mouth, but rather you are to speak it out your mouth. It should not be away from your lips at

any time. Continually speak it. Everyone knows how to mutter. To mutter means to speak things quietly or under your breath, speaking to yourself, regardless of whether people are present to hear you. You may mutter while you are driving your car, or maybe while you are shopping.[2]

The Hebrew word for *meditate* found in Joshua 1:8 is translated "to speak" in the following verses:

- "For the mouth shall speak [or meditate] truth" (Prov. 8:7, KJV).
- "And my tongue shall speak [or meditate] of thy righteousness and of thy praise all the day long" (Ps. 35:28, KJV).
- "The mouth of the righteous speaketh [meditate] wisdom, and his tongue talketh of judgment" (Ps. 37:30, KJV).

Dennis Burke has written a great book called *How to Meditate God's Word*. His teaching likens meditation to chewing the cud:

> To muse means to "ponder, consider, and study closely." This is the aspect of meditation that most people are aware of: taking hold of a promise or a truth and going over it again and again; not going over it in order to memorize it, but squeezing out all the richness; thinking on it and allowing it to wash through your inner man.
>
> The most vivid illustration I can give of musing is a cow chewing her cud. A cow grazes through the pasture, finds an abundance of tasty grass, chews it, and finally swallows it. Later, up comes the chewed grass to chew again (I know what you're thinking…but you have to admit—it is a good example!). Each time the cow brings up the old cud and chews it, she is refining it and making it more and more a part of her system. She chews all the

nutrients out of it; the stems and stalk are removed until
it is consumed into her body.

This is the most descriptive, powerful example of meditation. Treat the Word of God just as a cow chews her
cud. Feed on a scripture over and over again, swallow
it, then bring it back up again, going over it again and
again. Each time you chew on it, you are demanding all
the nutrients out of it, making it more and more a part
of your being.[3]

Animals that chew the cud will eat their food, swallow it, and
then bring it back up to re-chew it. In this way they get all of the
nutrients from what they eat and digest the food into their system
in a more complete way. Chewing is, of course, important to good
health and digestion. How many times have our parents told us to
chew our food completely?

Meditation is the process of chewing on the Word. We take a
scripture, speak it, think on it, and then we do it again. This is the
biblical way to get the Word into your system and to receive revelation and understanding. *To meditate* means "to ponder, regurgitate,
think aloud, consider continuously and utter something over and
over again."

This is exactly what we need to do with the Word of God.

> Not without significance, animals in the Old Testament
> were considered clean and suitable for food if they split
> the hoof and chewed the cud (Lev. 11:3). By analogy, we
> could say that a person who "chews the cud" in relation
> to God's word is *made clean and fruitful by the word*
> (John 15:3, 7); just as Christ's glorious church is cleansed
> by the washing of the water of the word (Eph. 5:26).[4]

> The cow is an animal with four compartments to its
> stomach, the largest of the four is the rumen, thus these

animals are called ruminants. Sheep, goats, bison and deer are other examples of ruminants and this information pertains to them also. The rumen acts somewhat like a large fermentation vat. Inside this vat are bacteria and protozoa that are cellulolytic, meaning they are able to digest cellulose, the major component of plant cell walls. The host animal, in this case the cow, provides the environment for these microbes and they in turn aid in digestion of plant components that the host could not otherwise utilize. These microbes also continue down the digestive tract of the animal where they are digested as part of the protein in the animal's diet. Monogastrics, or single stomached animals like humans and pigs don't have this symbiotic relationship going on to this extent and cannot make good use of the type of plants that cattle typically eat.

So in cattle, particles of food are bitten off, masticated to some extent and swallowed. Once a ruminant has eaten, it will go and peacefully stand or lie down while it "chews its cud". I say peacefully because if one is doing it's "cud chewing" it is at ease. The "cud" is actually a portion of regurgitated food that needs shredded into smaller particle for effective digestion in the rumen and beyond.[5]

Rumination—a cow chews something up and stores it up for later. The cow ruminates in perfect timing without waste. She squeezes the nourishment out of it. We transfer the life of Christ into us in a similar manner. This is so key in maintaining our deliverance!

The dictionary defines "meditate" as to "think about something deeply, to reflect on it or to ponder on it."

The definition of "muse" however, is not just to meditate on something but to comment upon it, to ruminate upon it—like a cow chewing the cud.[6]

"Meditate" or "muse"—Hebrew word *siyach*—means to put forth, meditate, muse, commune, speak, complain, ponder, sing, study, talk. Your meditation is also what you are speaking, muttering, singing, complaining about, or pondering.

> Give ear to my words, O Lord, consider my meditation.
>
> —Psalm 5:1

My meditation is connected to the words of my mouth.

> Let the words of my mouth, and the meditation of my heart, be acceptable in thy sight, O Lord, my strength, and my redeemer.
>
> —Psalm 19:14

> My mouth shall speak of wisdom; and the meditation of my heart shall be of understanding.
>
> —Psalm 49:3

My meditation should cause *gladness*.

> My meditation of him shall be sweet: I will be glad in the Lord.
>
> —Psalm 104:34, kjv

My meditation is on what I love.

> O how love I thy law! It is my meditation all the day.
>
> —Psalm 119:97, kjv

My meditation gives understanding.

> I have more understanding than all my teachers: for thy testimonies are my meditation.
>
> —Psalm 119:99, kjv

My meditation brings success.

> This book of the law shall not depart out of thy mouth; but thou shalt meditate therein day and night, that thou mayest observe to do according to all that is written therein: for then thou shalt make thy way prosperous, and then thou shalt have good success.
>
> —JOSHUA 1:8, KJV

My meditation is what I delight in.

> But his delight is in the law of the LORD; and in his law doth he meditate day and night.
>
> —PSALM 1:2, KJV

My meditation is at night.

> When I remember thee upon my bed, and meditate on thee in the night watches.
>
> —PSALM 63:6, KJV

MEDITATION UNCOVERS AND RELEASES GOD'S WISDOM

Joshua 1:8 is the only place the word *success* is found in the King James translation. Success is the Hebrew word *sakal*, meaning to be prudent, be circumspect, to act wisely, to understand, to prosper, give attention to, consider, ponder, to have insight, have comprehension, to act circumspectly, act prudently.[7]

We can see from this verse that meditation is connected to wisdom. Meditation will help you access the wisdom of God. The key to success is wisdom.

Wisdom is one of the greatest benefits of meditating in the Word of God.

> Wisdom is the principal thing; therefore get wisdom: and with all thy getting get understanding.
>
> —PROVERBS 4:7, KJV

The Good News Translation says it this way:

> Getting wisdom is the most important thing you can do.
> Whatever else you get, get insight.
>
> —Proverbs 4:7

Wisdom is best; wisdom is supreme. Wisdom is the first and primary thing you need to succeed in life.

> Happy is the man that findeth wisdom, and the man that getteth understanding. For the merchandise of it is better than the merchandise of silver, and the gain thereof than fine gold. She is more precious than rubies: and all the things thou canst desire are not to be compared unto her. Length of days is in her right hand; and in her left hand riches and honour. Her ways are ways of pleasantness, and all her paths are peace. She is a tree of life to them that lay hold upon her: and happy is every one that retaineth her.
>
> —Proverbs 3:13–18, kjv

These verses emphasize the value of wisdom. It is more precious than rubies. Nothing compares to wisdom. Wisdom results in long life. Wisdom brings you to riches and honor. Wisdom leads to peace. Wisdom promotes happiness. This is what biblical meditation will produce in your life. Wisdom produces riches and honor. Wisdom will cause you to inherit substance. Wisdom will fill your treasures. (See Proverbs 8:18–21.)

When you find wisdom, you will find life. You will obtain the favor of the Lord (Prov. 8:35). This is also in line with the benefits of being in covenant with God.

MEDITATING ON THE WORD BUILDS YOUR IMMUNITY AGAINST THE TRAPS OF THE ENEMY

When you are set free through deliverance, your spirit is made alive to the things of God. Meditation keeps you from falling back into a place of darkness and oppression that cuts you off from God. Meditation maintains your position of abiding in the vine—the place of fruitfulness and life. Meditation on the Word of God is also an act of constantly keeping before you the image and character of God. This brings life to your mortal body (Rom. 8:11) and keeps you in a constant state of getting stronger and becoming more alive in Christ. By contemplating the glory of God, we go from glory to glory and faith to faith (2 Cor. 3:18). By beholding, by meditating on God's Word, we become changed and immune to the traps of the enemy.

MEDITATION DECLARATIONS

I will meditate also of all the Lord's work and talk of His doings (Ps. 77:12).

I will meditate on the Lord's precepts and contemplate His ways (Ps. 119:15).

Princes also did sit and speak against me, but I meditate on the Lord's statutes (Ps. 119:23).

Let the proud be ashamed; for they dealt perversely with me without a cause: but I will meditate in thy precepts (Ps. 119:78).

My eyes are awake during the night watches, that I may meditate on the Lord's Word (Ps. 119:148).

I remember the days of old; I meditate on all thy works; I muse on the work of thy hands (Ps. 143:5).

I meditate upon these things; give myself wholly to them; that my profiting may appear to all (1 Tim. 4:15).

I love the law of the Lord; it is my meditation all the day (Ps. 119:97).

The law of the Lord is my delight, and in His law I meditate day and night (Ps. 1:2).

I shall be made to understand the way of the Lord's precepts, so I shall meditate on His wonderful works (Ps. 119:27).

I will remember the days of old and meditate on all the Lord's works. I will muse on the work of Your hands (Ps. 143:5).

I will lift my hands up to the Lord's commandments, which I love, and will meditate on His statutes (Ps. 119:48).

A book of remembrance will be written for me, who fears the Lord and meditates on His name (Mal. 3:16).

I will meditate on the book of the law day and night (Josh. 1:8).

THE BASICS OF DELIVERANCE[1]

A WAY FOR THE DELIVERANCE WORKER TO GET STARTED

1. Engage in brief conversations about the reason the person is there for ministry.

2. Engage in general prayer and worship—focus on God and His goodness, power, etc.

3. Bind powers over the area, break assignments from powers in the air to demons in the person. Ask for angelic protection (Heb. 1:14).

4. Ask and receive *by faith* the gifts of the Spirit needed to minister.

LEADERSHIP DURING DELIVERANCE TIME

1. Too many people commanding spirits (different ones) at the same time causes confusion for everyone, especially to the person being ministered to.

2. Leadership will often shift as the Holy Spirit directs.

3. Husbands are often the most effective in commanding spirits to leave their wives, with the support of others.

TACTICS OF SPEAKING TO DEMONS

1. Address the spirit by name, and if that is not known, address by function.

2. Either the Holy Spirit will give it, or the demon will reveal himself.

2. Do not rely on either method *exclusively*—be open to the Holy Spirit in this area.

3. Repeatedly remind these spirits that your authority is given to you by Jesus Christ, who is far above all rule and authority (Eph. 1:21).

4. Remind them of their fate in Revelation 20:10 and other places in Scripture (Job 30:3–8). Use the statement "The Lord Jesus Christ rebukes you" repeatedly, as a battering ram.

5. It is helpful to harass the demons to confess that Jesus Christ is their Lord.

6. Ruler demons often can be badgered for more information.

7. At times you will command the ruler demon to go and then clean out the lesser demons under him, and if that does not work, reverse the tactics.

8. Bind and separate interfering spirits as God leads.

9. There is no need to shout at demons since the battle is not in the flesh but in the spirit.

WHAT TO EXPECT IN RECEIVING DELIVERANCE

While many deliverances involve obvious physical manifestations, not all react in this manner. Some spirits leave quietly and nonviolently.

You may not have a strong physical reaction when receiving deliverance; therefore, don't be disappointed if you don't receive in this manner. What you should expect is a release. You know there is a release when...

1. Oppressive force disappears.

2. Heaviness lifts.

3. Uneasiness goes away.

4. Burden or load lightens.

5. There is an inner sense of liberty, freedom, and divine satisfaction or contentment.

6. The joy of the Lord comes, and you are able to rejoice.

The result of deliverance is "righteousness, peace and joy in the Holy Ghost" (Rom. 14:17, KJV). When devils are cast out, *the kingdom of God has come* (Matt. 12:28).

DEMON MANIFESTATIONS

When evil spirits depart, you can normally expect some sort of manifestation through the mouth or nose. Listed below are some of the common manifestations:

1. Coughing

2. Drooling

3. Vomiting

4. Spitting

5. Foaming

6. Crying

7. Screaming

8. Sighing

9. Roaring

10. Belching

11. Yawning

12. Exhaling

Again, when demons are cast out, they normally leave through the mouth or nose. Spirits are associated with breathing. Both the Hebrews and the Greeks had only one word for *spirit* and *breath*. In the Greek the word is *pneuma*. The Holy Spirit is breathed *in* (John 20:22). Evil spirits are breathed *out*.

Sometimes people shake or tremble when they receive deliverance. Their body, in whole or part, may actually shake or tremble.

HINDRANCES TO RECEIVING DELIVERANCE

1. Curses

2. Sin

3. Pride

4. Passivity

5. Ungodly soul ties

6. Occultism

7. Fear

8. Embarrassment

9. Unbelief

10. Lack of desire

11. Unforgiveness

12. Lack of knowledge

In many cases demons have legal, biblical grounds. They may not torment at will. If demons have legal grounds, they have the right to remain. These legal grounds must be destroyed in order to receive and maintain deliverance. There are other cases demons will try to operate illegally. Believers can experience illegal attacks and therefore need to use their authority. In other words, demons will try to take advantage of ignorance, and believers need to have knowledge of their covenant rights and walk in them by faith.

How to Keep Your Deliverance

1. Read God's Word daily.

2. Find a group of Bible-believing people, preferably a church, and regularly meet with them for worship, study, and ministry.

3. Pray with the understanding and in tongues.

4. Place the blood of Jesus on yourself and your family.

5. Determine as nearly as you can which spirits have been cast out of you. Make a list for these areas Satan will try to recapture.

6. The way demons gain reentry is through a lax, undisciplined thought life. The mind is the battlefield. You must cast down imaginations and bring every thought into the obedience of Christ (2 Cor. 10:5).

7. Pray to the Father fervently, asking Him to make you alert, sober, and vigilant against wrong thoughts (1 Pet. 5:8–9).

8. The demons signal their approach to you by the fact that the old thought patterns you once had are now trying to return unto you. As soon as this happens, immediately

rebuke them. State *verbally* that you refuse them as quickly as possible.

9. You have the authority to loose the *angels of the Lord* to battle the demons. (See Hebrews 1:14; Matthew 18:18.) Bind the demons and loose upon them the spirits of destruction (1 Chron. 21:12) and burning the judgment (Isa. 4:4) from the Lord Jesus Christ. Also, loose warrior angels upon the demons.

NOTES

CHAPTER 1
DELIVERANCE AND THE COVENANT OF MERCY

1. Blue Letter Bible, s.v. "*checed*," http://www.blueletterbible.org/ lang/lexicon/lexicon.cfm?Strongs=H2617&t=WEB (accessed December 4, 2013).
2. Blue Letter Bible, s.v. "*racham*," http://www.blueletterbible.org/ lang/lexicon/lexicon.cfm?Strongs=H7355&t=WEB (accessed December 4, 2013).
3. Merriam-Webster Online, s.v. "endure," http://www.merriam -webster.com/dictionary/endure (accessed December 4, 2013).
4. Merriam-Webster Online, s.v. "forever," http://www.merriam -webster.com/dictionary/forever (accessed December 4, 2013).

CHAPTER 2
DELIVERANCE IS THE CHILDREN'S BREAD

1. Merriam-Webster Online, s.v. "sustenance," http://www.merriam -webster.com/dictionary/sustenance (accessed December 4, 2013).
2. Merriam-Webster Online, s.v. "staple," http://www.merriam -webster.com/dictionary/staple (accessed December 4, 2013).
3. Merriam-Webster Online, s.v. "principal," http://www.merriam -webster.com/dictionary/principal (accessed December 4, 2013).
4. R. K. Harrison, *The Psalms for Today* (Grand Rapids, MI: Zondervan, 1961), as quoted in Curtis Vaughn, ed., *The Word: The Bible From 26 Translations* (N.p.: Mathis Publishers, 1991).

CHAPTER 3
REJECTION: THE DOORWAY TO DEMONIC OPPRESSION

1. Noel and Phyl Gibson, *Excuse Me, Your Rejection Is Showing* (N.p.: Sovereign World Ltd., 2008).
2. Blue Letter Bible, s.v. "*ekballō*," http://www.blueletterbible.org/ lang/lexicon/lexicon.cfm?Strongs=G1544&t=KJV (accessed December 5, 2013).

Chapter 4
"Loose Thyself"—Self-Deliverance

1. See Frank and Ida Mae Hammond's *Pigs in the Parlor* (Kirkwood, MO: Impact Christian Books, 1973), 57.
2. Merriam-Webster Online, s.v. "trauma," http://www.merriam-webster.com/dictionary/trauma (accessed December 5, 2013).

Chapter 7
Meditate on the Word to Maintain Your Deliverance

1. Peter Tan, *Meditation on God's Word* (Belconnen, Australia: Peter Tan Evangelism, 2008), 4, http://spiritword.net/ebooks/Foundational_Truth01.pdf (accessed December 10, 2013).
2. Dennis Burke, *How to Meditate God's Word* (Arlington, TX: Dennis Burke Publications, 1982).
3. Ibid. Permission requested.
4. Olive Tree Learning Center, "Meditating on God's Word," http://www.olivetree.com/learn/articles/meditating-on-gods-word.php (accessed December 10, 2013). Emphasis added.
5. Greenvistafarm.com, "Animal Benefits: Animal Benefits of a 100% Forage Diet," http://www.greenvistafarm.com/animal.html (accessed December 10, 2013).
6. Tom Smith, "Discovering the Lost Art of Musing on the Word of God," Holdingtotruth.com, http://holdingtotruth.com/2012/05/07/discovering-the-lost-art-of-musing-on-the-word-of-god/ (accessed December 10, 2013).
7. Blue Letter Bible, "Dictionary and Word Seaerch for *sakal* (Strong's 7919)," http://www.blueletterbible.org/lang/lexicon/lexicon.cfm?Strongs=H7919&t=KJV (accessed December 10, 2013).

Appendix
The Basics of Deliverance

1. Adapted from Win Worley, *Annihilating the Hosts of Hell* (N.p.: H.B.C., 1981). Permission requested.

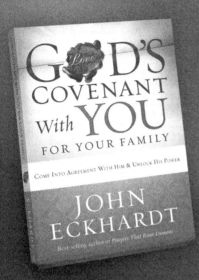